STUDIES IN GENESIS ONE

EDWARD J. YOUNG

PUBLISHING
P.O. BOX 817 • PHILLIPSBURG • NEW JERSEY 08865-0817

DEDICATED
TO

OSWALD T. ALLIS

who has so greatly influenced my
thinking on the Old Testament

Library of Congress Catalogue Card Number 64–17028

.

Printed in the United States of America

CONTENTS

EDITOR'S PREFACE

THE history of the doctrine of inspiration of Scripture gives evidence that the subordination of biblical authority to reason, to feelings, or to science invariably leads to mistrust of more and more biblical teachings. One cannot help being concerned about the drift of some evangelical scholars to subject the interpretation of Genesis 1 to modern scientific opinions. There is a dangerous tendency to interpret the first chapter of Genesis, not by strict and accurate exegesis, but in a manner so as to satisfy the "scientific mind." This yielding spirit is fraught with danger not only to the biblical doctrine of creation but to other doctrines as well.

The Christian theologian must always subject his mind to the authority of Scripture, and his primary concern must be to interpret the infallible Word according to the intended meaning of the writer. This may expose the interpreter to the scorn of the modern scholar, but it is the only honest method for those who hold unequivocally to the biblical concept of inspiration. Not only the authority of the Old Testament is at stake but also that of the New Testament, for it looks upon the revelation of Genesis 1 as an account of historical facts.

Evangelical and Reformed scholarship has been especially blessed with competent scholars in the Old Testament field. Men like Robert Dick Wilson and Oswald T. Allis have been mighty defenders of the faith and distinguished scholars. A worthy successor is Professor Edward J. Young of Westminster Theological Seminary of Philadelphia. His written works have earned him the reputation of being the leading conservative scholar in the field of Old Testament today. The present treatise on the first chapter of Genesis reveals both a depth of learning and a spirit willing to subject itself to the authority of the Word.

Among the published works of Dr. Young are: *The Prophecy of Daniel; An Introduction to the Old Testament; Thy Word Is Truth;* and his most recent, *Commentary on Isaiah.*

J. Marcellus Kik, *Editor*

PREFACE

THE following three studies in the first chapter of Genesis are based upon the assumption that this chapter is a revelation from God, and that it tells us about the origin of all things. It is not regarded as the product of the mature reflection of the Israelites, nor as an account devised by the faith and thought of Israel of old.

This position runs counter to much that is being written in the present day, but much that is written today is based upon a view of the Bible which is not that of the Bible itself. In these three studies I have simply endeavored to take the Bible as it stands, and sought to interpret its first chapter. In so doing I wish to make it plain that I am no foe of science, but I believe that the facts of the created universe, when rightly interpreted, will prove to be in harmony with the revelation which God has given us in the first chapter of Genesis. Without this first chapter of the Bible, our endeavors to explain the origin of all things will be futile, for this chapter contains information which we cannot find elsewhere.

It is my sincere hope that the study of these articles, which first appeared in the *Westminster Theological Journal,* will at least cause men to entertain a higher view of the trustworthiness of the first chapter of Genesis than is often the case and will lead them to a greater reverence and love for Him who is the Creator of heaven and earth.

March 1964   Edward J. Young

THE RELATION OF THE FIRST VERSE
OF GENESIS ONE TO VERSES TWO
AND THREE

IF THE first chapter of Genesis presents an historical account of the creation, it follows that, for a proper understanding of the chapter, one must also apprehend the relationship in which the first verse stands to the following. If, on the other hand, the chapter contains mere mythology or untrustworthy tradition or is not to be regarded as historical, the exegetical questions which it raises are of comparatively minor importance. The following attempt to discuss the relationship in which the first verse of Genesis stands to the following is based upon the assumption that these verses present a factual account of what actually occurred.

Is GENESIS I:I A DEPENDENT CLAUSE?

We may first note those interpretations which do not consider the verse an independent statement, but treat it as a dependent clause, with the principal or independent sentence following.

1. Ibn Ezra and others regarded the first verse as a dependent clause, the main statement appearing in verse two.[1] The thought would then be, "When God began to create the heaven and the earth, the earth was without form and void".

2. A second view finds the first verse to be a dependent statement, with verse two a parenthesis, the main thought

---

[1] If this construction of Ibn Ezra's were correct, we should expect verse two to read, ותהי הארץ or היתה הארץ. Thus, in Jeremiah 26:1 we read, בראשית ממלכות יהויקים ... היה הדבר הזה and in Hosea 1:2, תחלת דבר יהוה בהושע ויאמר יהוה אל הושע. See U. Cassuto: *A Commentary On The Book of Genesis* (in Hebrew), 1953, Part I, p. 10.

2

being expressed in the third verse.[2] On this construction we may render, "When God began to create the heaven and the earth — and the earth was without form and void, etc. — then God said, 'Let there be light' ". One of the first to propound this view was Rashi, and he has had many followers. These two views are probably the most important of those which regard the first verse as a dependent statement. And of the two it is the latter which is by far the more widely accepted today.[3] Each of these two interpretations constitutes a serious departure from the traditional position that the first verse is an independent statement. It must be clearly seen that if verse one is a dependent clause, the doctrine of absolute creation is then not taught in the first chapter of Genesis.[4] On either of these constructions, when the work indicated by בָּרָא is begun, there is already in existence material which may be designated הָאָרֶץ, albeit that material was an uninhabitable mass. Pre-existing matter was there at hand, and, consequently, whatever else בָּרָא may then mean, in the nature of the case it cannot denote absolute creation. At best it would have to indicate some work of moulding or forming. Inasmuch, however, as the material which God is to employ is already at hand — how it came to be there

[2] Cassuto points out (op. cit., p. 10) that if this construction were correct we should expect to find in verse two, והארץ תהו ובהו, and the היתה should be omitted. Thus, in I Samuel 3:2 ff., the circumstantial clauses are expressed וּשְׁמוּאֵל שֹׁכֵב and וְעֵלִי שֹׁכֵב.

[3] This construction is adopted in *The Bible, An American Translation* (The University of Chicago Press, 1931), p. 3. Genesis is translated by Theophile J. Meek. *The Westminster Study Edition of the Holy Bible* (The Westminster Press, Philadelphia, 1948), p. 23, in a footnote, prefers this construction to the more accurate rendering of the Authorized Version. It also appears in the translation of James Moffatt (Doubleday, Doran & Company, Inc., Garden City, New York, 1922), p. 1. Hermann Gunkel (*Die Genesis*, Göttingen, 1922), p. 101, places 2:4a before verse one, as does August Dillmann (*Genesis Critically and Exegetically Expounded*, Edinburgh, 1897, p. 55).

[4] As is the case in the Revised Standard Version, the Westminster Study Edition renders one way in the body of the text and then, without further explanation, suggests the other (namely, that verse one is a dependent clause) in a footnote. Such a procedure can only confuse the unlearned reader and awaken a doubt in his mind as to the reliability of the text of the Old Testament.

we are not told — God's activity mentioned in verse one would not be that of true creation. It is necessary that we fully realize the implications involved in the acceptance of either of these views. Our acceptance or rejection of a particular interpretation must, of course, depend upon exegetical considerations, but we must also be guided by the analogy of Scripture. If then we are to adopt either of these views we must be clear as to what we are doing and of the consequences involved, and whatever we do, we must not follow the practice of those who seem to imply that Genesis 1:1 can at the same time be either a dependent or an independent statement.[5] Are we then on safe exegetical ground if we assert that absolute creation is not taught in the first chapter of Genesis?

GENESIS 1:1 — AN INDEPENDENT CLAUSE

Those who interpret Genesis 1:1 as a dependent clause construe בְּרֵאשִׁית as a construct. Some, such as *Biblia Hebraica*, then suggest that the verb בָּרָא be emended to the infinitive construct בְּרֹא, so that the translation would be, "in the beginning of the creating of God", *i. e.*, "when God began to create".[6] It is not necessary, however, to emend the word, because the construct followed by a finite verb is a genuine Semitic usage.[7] If the finite verb be retained

---

[5] With respect to the significance of Genesis 1:1 if taken as a temporal clause, Gunkel (*op. cit.*, p. 102) remarks, "Beide (*i. e.*, either the construction of Genesis 1:1 as an independent statement or as a temporal clause) sind übrigens nur grammatisch und nicht dem Sinne nach verschieden". This statement must be dismissed as incorrect.

[6] *Biblia Hebraica*, ed. Rud. Kittel (Privileg. Württ. Bibelanstalt, 1954), *ad loc.*

[7] There are numerous biblical examples of this construction. *Cf.* Lev. 14:46; I Sam. 5:9; 25:15; Ps. 16:3; 58:9; 81:6; Isa. 29:1; Hos. 1:2. As the following examples will show, the construct in Babylonian may also be followed by a finite verb. a-wa-at iq-bu-ú, "the word which he has spoken," *Code of Hammurabi*, col. Va:62; na-di-in id-di-nušum, "the seller who sold to him", col. VIIa: 19, 20; bīt ipušu imqut, "(when) the house which he built falls", col. XIX: 69 f.; bīt imqutu ippeš, "the house which fell, he built", col. XIX:92; ina dīn idīnu, "in the judgment which he has judged", col. VI:15. Von Soden gives several examples: ana bīt tērubu damiqta šukun, "procure good for the house (in which) thou didst enter", kasap

4

the rendering would be "In the beginning of God created —"
i e., "When God began to create".

It will first be necessary to ascertain whether in this particular passage בְּרֵאשִׁית must be construed as a construct. All told the word רֵאשִׁית is found 50 times in the Old Testament. Apart from Genesis 1:1 the form בְּרֵאשִׁית appears only four times, always in Jeremiah and in each instance in the construct state. For that matter the greater number of occurrences of the word are clearly in the construct.[8]

As has often been pointed out, the word serves to designate the first or best part of a thing. Thus, in Genesis 10:10, the words, "the beginning of his kingdom was Asshur", would not signify that the kingdom began with Asshur, but rather that Asshur was its center and core. The beginning of the first fruits (e g., Deuteronomy 26:1) was their best part. From this the word easily came to have a temporal significance, namely, the first part of something. Thus the phrase, "In the beginning of the reign of Jehoiakim" (Jeremiah 26:1), has reference to the earliest stages of that reign.

There are, however, some passages in which רֵאשִׁית does stand in the absolute state. In Isaiah 46:10, even though it does not necessarily refer to the absolute beginning, the word is nevertheless in the absolute state. Likewise in Nehemiah 12:44 the word is clearly in the absolute. If then we sum up the occurrences of רֵאשִׁית in the Old Testament, we find that whereas there are some examples of the absolute, for the most part the word is found in the construct. As far as the form itself is concerned one cannot tell whether it is absolute or construct. This decision must be based upon other considerations.

ērišū-ka, "the silver which he asked of thee" (*Grundriss der Akkadischen Grammatik*, 1952, p. 219). Von Soden comments, "Rel.-S. können auch ohne einleitendes Rel. Pron. unmittelbar an das Beziehungssubst. angeschlossen werden; dieses tritt dann wie vor einer nominalen Gen. in den St. cstr" (p. 219).

[8] An excellent recent discussion of the significance of רֵאשִׁית will be found in N. H. Ridderbos: "Genesis i 1 und 2", in *Oudtestamentische Studiën*, Deel xii, *Studies on the Book of Genesis*, 1958, pp. 216–219. His conclusion is that the use of רֵאשִׁית in Genesis 1:1 does not support the translation of the first verse as a temporal clause.

5

1. In the Masoretic text בְּרֵאשִׁית is accented with the disjunctive Tiphcha. This means that according to the Masoretes the word has its own independent accent. The Masoretes therefore evidently construed the word as an absolute. This, of course, is not a decisive consideration, for the Masoretes were not infallible; but it has its place.
2. Likewise of significance is the fact that with no exceptions the ancient versions construed בְּרֵאשִׁית as an absolute.[9]

[9] It is interesting to note that certain recent commentaries likewise do not treat the first verse as a temporal clause. J. Chaine: *Le Livre de la Genèse*, 1949, "Au commencement Elohim créa les cieux et la terre". Chaine comments, "affirmation globale qui veut dire que Dieu est l'auteur du monde. Après cette indication qui résume en une formule toute l'oeuvre de Dieu, l'auteur reprend les choses plus en détail" (pp. 21, 22). *La Sainte Bible*, Tome I, 1er Partie, *Genèse* (Paris, 1953), translates, "Au commencement Dieu créa le ciel et la terre". With respect to the translation of verse one as a temporal clause, we read, "Les raisons invoquées a l'appui de cette interprétation, entres autres la construction prétendue semblable de II, 4b, et celle de récits babyloniens ne sauraient prévaloir contre le caractère même du récit aux phrases courtes se continuant et se complétant" (p. 104). Walther Zimmerli: *1. Mose 1–11, Die Urgeschichte*, 1943, renders, "Im Anfang schuf Gott den Himmel und die Erde" (p. 23). Alan Richardson: *Genesis I-XI*, 1953, renders the verse in the traditional manner; Karlheinz Rabast: *Die Genesis*, 1951, adopts the traditional rendering of the verse and also remarks, "בְּרֵאשִׁית steht ohne Artikel im Verbalsatz betont voran; es wird deshalb stat. abs. sein" (p. 43). We may also mention H. C. Leupold: *Exposition of Genesis*, 1942; U. Cassuto: *op. cit.*, p. 10, who remarks, יש להסיק שהפסוק הראשון עומד בפני עצמו and Gerhard Von Rad: *Das erste Buch Mose*, 1952, pp. 36, 37. Appeal for taking verse one as a temporal clause is sometimes made to the so-called creation account of Babylonia, *Enuma Elish*. In discussing this question, Heidel points out that if the writer of Genesis had patterned his account on the old Mesopotamian documents, it is strange that he should have employed בְּרֵאשִׁית instead of בְּיוֹם. See Alexander Heidel: *The Babylonian Genesis* (Chicago, 1951), pp. 95 ff. The old Greek translations give βαρασήθ, βαρησέθ, βρησίθ, βρισήθ and βρησίδ (cf. Field: *Origenis Hexaplorum quae supersunt*, Vol. I, Oxford 1875, p. 7). These variations, however, do not necessarily support the reading בְּרֵאשִׁית. Procksch: *Die Genesis*, 1924, p. 440, remarks, "absolut zu fassen, wie auch das masoretische Tiphcha bestimmt". "Bei solchen unbestimmten Zeitbegriffen fehlt der Artikel gern". Eduard König: *Die Genesis*, Gütersloh, 1925, "Diese absolute Auffassung von *bereschith* ist neuerdings also mit Recht auch von folgenden vertreten worden: Wellhausen, Proleg.[2] 411; Delitzsch; Strack; Spurrell; Driver; Gunkel 1910, 102

6

3. In the Old Testament when a construct precedes a finite verb that fact is apparent either from the form of the word in construct or from the fact that the context demands that the word be taken as a construct. In Hosea 1:2, for example, we read תְּחִלַּת דִּבֶּר יהוה. Here the form of the word shows clearly that תְּחִלַּת must be a construct. On the other hand in a phrase such as that found in Exodus 6:28, וַיְהִי בְּיוֹם דִּבֶּר the context demands that, although as far as the form is concerned it might be either absolute or construct, יוֹם be taken in the construct state.[10]

In Genesis 1:1 neither of these conditions is present. Neither the form of the word nor the context demands that בְּרֵאשִׁית be taken as a construct. In fact, as we shall seek to point out, the context not only does not demand the construct but, if anything, favors the use of the absolute.

We may approach a consideration of this context by noting the alliteration with which the Bible begins. The sequence ברא of בראשית appears again in the verb בָּרָא. This would seem to tie up the concept expressed by בְּרֵאשִׁית with that of בָּרָא. What then is the significance of בָּרָא? This question can be answered only by a survey of its usage in the Old Testament, and such a survey will confirm the time-honored and oft-noted view. In the Qal stem בָּרָא is employed exclusively of the divine activity. The subject of the verb is always God and never man. The idea of novelty or extraordinariness of result seems frequently to be implied. The word is employed with the accusative of the product but the

allerdings mehr bloss dem Scheine nach; Procksch 1913, 425; F. Kauleń, Der bibl. Schöpfungsbericht (1902), 9; Vinc. Zapletal, Der Schöpfungsbericht (1902), 8; J. Nikel, Genesis und Keilschriftforschung (1903), 107; Murillo'', (p. 134).

Wellhausen speaks of the construction of verse one as a temporal clause as "verzweifelt" (*Prolegomena*,⁵ p. 386).

[10] This argument has been elaborated by G. Ch. Aalders: *De Goddelijke Openbaring in de eerste drie Hoofdstukken van Genesis*, 1932, p. 206, "Wanneer men nagaat, in welke gevallen een zelfstandig naamwoord *in statu constructo* met een verbogen werkwoordvorm verbonden wordt, ziet men onveranderlijk, dat alle misverstand is uitgesloten, hetzij omdat aan den vorm van het zelfstandig naamwoord te zien is dat het *status constructus* is ... hetzij omdat de zin en het zinsverband slechts één mogelijkheid toelaten''.

material used, if any, is never mentioned. We are told that God created (בָּרָא) man, for example, but we are never told that God created man from the dust of the ground.[11]

The word בָּרָא therefore, has a more restricted usage than does the English word "create". If in Genesis 1:1 Moses desired to express the thought of absolute creation there was no more suitable word in the Hebrew language at his disposal. And when this word is taken in close conjunction with בְּרֵאשִׁית we may paraphrase the thought, "The beginning was by means of a creative act". The beginning and unique creation — namely, that of heaven and earth — are here joined together. Hence, we may understand the writer as asserting that the heaven and earth had a beginning and that this beginning is to be found in the fact that God had created them.

The first verse of Genesis therefore stands as a simple declaration of the fact of absolute creation. When we consider the universe, and the questions arise in our minds, "Who made these things? What was their origin?" the first verse of Genesis gives an answer. And it answers with the simple declaration that God created the heaven and the earth.

THE FIRST THREE VERSES OF GENESIS

What, however, is the relationship in which verse one stands to the following? An approach to the answer of this question can be found by an examination of the nature of verse two. The second verse consists of three circumstantial clauses:

1. "and the earth was desolation and waste",
2. "and darkness — upon faces of abyss",
3. "and the Spirit of God — brooding upon faces of the waters".

---

[11] The usage of the word has been discussed by Ridderbos (*op. cit.*, pp. 219–223) who also comments on some of the recent literature. Rabast (*op. cit.*) sums up the usage as follows: "Das Verbum wird nur vom Schaffen Gottes gebraucht, niemals vom Tun des Menschen; es bedeutet immer, dass Gott etwas Wunderbares, Neues hervorbringt; es hat nie ein Objekt des Stoffes bei sich. Gott schafft völlig anders als ein Mensch" (p. 43).

In the Semitic languages a circumstantial clause is descriptive of a particular condition, and is therefore to be distinguished from a narrative clause.[12] The narrative clause contains a finite verb, whereas the circumstantial clause does not. Verse two contains three circumstantial clauses, thus describing a three-fold set of circumstances or conditions which were in existence at a particular time. The particular time in which this three-fold condition was present is to be determined by the finite verb, with which these three clauses are to be construed.

There would seem to be two grammatical possibilities. In the first place the three clauses might be construed with the בָּרָא of verse one.[13] If that were the case, the meaning would be that when God began the activity expressed by בָּרָא the three-fold condition described in verse two was already present. How long it had been present before God began to create, we would not know. We should simply be told that when God began to create, there was the world before him, desolation and waste, covered with darkness and water, the Spirit brooding upon it. The work expressed by בָּרָא, whatever else it might be, could not be that of absolute creation.

Although such a construction is gramatically possible, it is to be rejected as unsuitable to the context. The significance of בָּרָא when taken in connection with בְּרֵאשִׁית, together with the emphasis upon the divine monergism, as well as the progress of thought in the chapter make it clear that the

---

[12] For a discussion of the nature and function of the circumstantial clause in Hebrew, cf. Gesenius' Hebrew Grammar, Second English Edition, revised by A. E. Cowley, 1910, pp. 451, 489; William Henry Green: A Grammar of The Hebrew Language, 1898, pp. 377–379; H. S. Nyberg: Hebreisk Grammatik, 1952, pp. 283 ff.; P. Paul Joüon, Grammaire de l'Hébreu Biblique, 1947, p. 487.

[13] This view is adopted by Unger ("Rethinking The Genesis Account Of Creation" in Bibliotheca Sacra, Vol. 115, No. 457, p. 28) who says, "In the original language Genesis 1:2 consists of three circumstantial clauses, all describing conditions or circumstances existing *at the time of* the principal action indicated in verse 1, or giving a reason for that action". Unger does not refer Genesis 1:1–3 to the original creation but to a later work of God, namely, the refashioning of a "judgment ridden" earth in preparation for man. He translates verse one, "In the beginning God fashioned (or formed) the heavens and the earth". As we shall seek to show, this construction does not do justice to the language of Genesis.

chapter is not concerned merely with the reformation of already existing material.[14] Its theme is far grander than that.

The second possibility is to construe the three circumstantial clauses with the verb וַיֹּאמֶר of verse three.[15] We may then paraphrase, "At the time when God said, 'Let there be light', a three-fold condition was in existence, namely, *etc.*".

On this construction we are not told how long this three-fold condition had been in existence, whether for years or merely for moments. Nor is the creation of the three-fold condition explicitly stated. But we are now in a position to understand the relationship of verse one to what follows.

The first verse of Genesis is a broad, general, declaration of the fact of the creation of the heaven and the earth. The terms אֵת הַשָּׁמַיִם וְאֵת הָאָרֶץ include all things.[16] When the child asks its parent, "Who made the world?" his question has reference to the world as he sees it. And when the parent replies, "God made the world", the parent does not intend to deny that God made the original material from which the present arrangement of the world is formed. Likewise, the first verse of Genesis, while telling us that the universe as we now know it was created by God, does not at all exclude the thought that the original material from which this present universe was fashioned, was also created by God.[17] That fact

[14] *Cf.* Young: "Genesis One And Natural Science" in *Torch and Trumpet*, Vol. VII, No. 4, pp. 16, 17.

[15] There are several examples in the Old Testament of circumstantial clauses which precede the verb with which they are to be construed, *e. g.*, Gen. 38:25; Num. 12:14; Josh. 2:18; I Sam. 9:11; I Kings 14:17; II Kings 2:23; 6:5, 26; 9:25; Job 1:16; Isa. 37:38.

[16] *Cf.* Cyrus H. Gordon: *The World of the Old Testament*, New York, 1958, pp. 35–37.

[17] A number of commentators have insisted that the phrase "the heaven and the earth" refers to the primaeval material from which the universe was developed. Calvin asserts that the world was created "an empty chaos of heaven and earth," and seems to derive this thought from the words heaven and earth. "Simpliciter enim hoc voluit Moses: non statim ab initio expolitum fuisse mundum, ut hodie cernitur, sed inane coeli et terrae chaoe fuisse creatum" *Calvini Opera Quae Supersunt Omnia*, Brunsvigiae, 1882, vol. xxiii, p. 14.

Aalders: *Het Boek Genesis*, Eerste Deel, 1949, p. 77 (De Korte Verklaring der Heilige Schrift) argues that the manner in which verse two is connected to verse one shows that verse one is not a simple heading. Consequently, he asserts, the phrase הַשָּׁמַיִם וְהָאָרֶץ of verse one does not designate the

is stated in grand summary fashion in verse one. Then follows a detailed account of how God brought the well-

well ordered universe, but rather the condition of the world before God began his work of fashioning it into its present form ("moet dus de aanduiding wezen van de wereld voor de nadere vorming en ordening welke in die verzen wordt getekend" p. 78). It is the substance of heaven and earth ("in Gen. 1:1 wordt beschreven de schepping van de stof waaruit de ganse wereld is gevormd" p. 78).

In answer it should be noted that elsewhere, as Aalders himself seems to acknowledge (see the discussion on p. 75 with the references adduced) the phrase הַשָּׁמַיִם וְהָאָרֶץ does designate the well-ordered universe, ὁ κόσμος. Secondly, the conclusions which Aalders draws from the connection between verses one and two do not necessarily follow. Verse two does obviously connect with verse one and employs the word הָאָרֶץ in a sense different from that which it had in the first verse. In verse two הָאָרֶץ serves as a practical equivalent of our designation "the earth." It is the earth as we now know it (cf. Procksch: op. cit., p. 441, "die bekannte Erde"). Hence, the thought may be paraphrased as follows: "And the earth (i. e., the earth we now know) at that time was desolation and waste." Aalders also interprets the הָאָרֶץ of verse two in a similar fashion, "Dat de aarde hier zo op den voorgrond treedt behoeft geen verwondering te wekken: zij is het, waarop wij mensen wonen, waarop wij leven, lijden en sterven" (p. 78). Dr. Aalders also, then, is forced to take the word הָאָרֶץ in verse two in a different sense from that which he gave to it is verse one. In verse one he took it in connection with הַשָּׁמַיִם as signifying the primaeval world material; in verse two he refers it to the world on which men now live. That verse two refers to verse one does not therefore prove that verse one must have the meaning which Dr. Aalders gives to it.

We may note also the following; "Quae coeli terraeque nomine in hoc Versu primo eorum tantummodo designatur materia, quae omnium primum erat efficienda" (Rosenmüller: Scholia In Vetus Testamentum, Partis Primae Volumen Primum, Lipsiae, MDCCCXXI, p. 64); C. F. Keil and F. Delitzsch: Biblical Commentary On The Old Testament, Vol. I, 1949, p. 48. August Knobel (Die Genesis, Leipzig, 1852, pp. 7, 8) remarks, "d. h. den Anfang des Schaffens damit gemacht, dass er den Weltstoff hervorbrachte." With respect to the words "heaven and earth" he comments that they apply "—auf die chaotische Masse mit dem sie umgebenden Raume, also auf den Weltstoff" (p. 8). Skinner is correct in his comment (A Critical And Exegetical Commentary on Genesis, New York, 1925, p. 14) "For though that phrase (i. e., the heavens and the earth) is a Hebrew designation of the universe as a whole, it is only the organised universe, not the chaotic material out of which it was formed, that can actually be so designated." Gunkel comments (op. cit., p. 102), "Auf keinen Fall aber ist es erlaubt . . . וְהָאָרֶץ הַשָּׁמַיִם als Bezeichnung der urzeitigen, noch chaotischen Welt zu verstehen und zu behaupten, Vers 1

11

ordered universe from the original material into its present form. In this detailed account, however, there is no explicit statement of the creation of the primeval material from which the universe we know was formed. The first act in forming the present universe was God's speaking. The verb וַיֹּאמֶר is introduced by *waw* consecutive, but it should now be clear that וַיֹּאמֶר is not the second verb in a series introduced by בָּרָא of verse one.[18] Verse one is a narrative complete in itself. Verses 2–31 likewise constitute a narrative complete in itself. In this narrative the first verb is וַיֹּאמֶר. No previous verb in the perfect appears.

In a narrative in the past time we often find the first verb in the perfect and each succeeding verb in the imperfect with *waw* consecutive. The first verb, however, *i. e.*, the verb in the perfect, need not be expressed. Such is the case in the narrative comprised by verses 2–31. The first action mentioned in this narrative is that of the וַיֹּאמֶר of verse three.

It has already been stated that we are not told how long the three-fold condition described in verse two had been in existence before God said, "Let there be light". In view of the immediately preceding statement of absolute creation, however, we may not be far wrong if we assume that this three-fold condition had been in existence from the very beginning until God said, "Let there be light". How long a time that was we of course have no means of knowing. Verse two then states the condition of the earth as it was when created and until God began to form from it the present world.

Was, then, this three-fold condition a chaos? There are those who say that it was. What, however, is a chaos? As

enthalte die Schöpfung der Welt als Chaos (so Wellhausen, Prolegomena⁶ 296, Composition³ 105), wobei dann Vers 2 den chaotischen Zustand dieser ersten Schöpfung und erst 3ff. die Entstehung der gegenwärtigen geordneten Welt schildern müsste."

[18] A similarly constructed narrative is found in I Kings 18:30 ff. Verse 30b is the general statement of the repairing of the altar. The detailed account begins in verse 31. The first verb in the detailed account is וַיִּקַּח (verse 31). Grammatically, this verb does not follow וַיְרַפֵּא of verse 30. The order of thought is not, "First, Elijah repaired the altar, and then he took twelve stones." Verse 30b is a narrative unit, complete in itself; verses 31 ff. constitute another narrative unit, the first verb of which is וַיִּקַּח.

one of his definitions Webster states that chaos is, "The void and formless infinite; the confused, unorganized state of primordial matter before the creation of distinct or orderly forms; — sometimes personified, after the Greeks, as the most ancient of the Gods".[19] In the Greek language the word χαός was used of the first state of the universe which was sometimes thought to be water, sometimes unformed matter.[20]

It is occasionally said that the statement, "creation of a chaos", would involve a contradiction in terms,[21] and hence, it is concluded that verse two does not present the condition of things as they came from the hand of the Creator.[22]

If, however, instead of asking, without more precisely defining the term, whether verse two describes a chaos, we simply seek to ascertain just what verse two does teach, we shall be in a better position to answer the question whether the world could have been created as it is pictured in verse two.

We are first told that the earth was תֹהוּ וָבֹהוּ, desolation and waste. The significance of תֹהוּ is clearly illustrated by Isaiah 45:18, where it is set in contrast with לָשָׁבֶת. The purpose of creating the world is said to be that it might be inhabited, not that it might be תֹהוּ.[23] תֹהוּ, therefore, indicates the world as desolate and uninhabitable.[24] Together with בֹהוּ it forms a striking phrase. בֹהוּ has essentially the

---

[19] *Webster's New International Dictionary*, Springfield, 1946.

[20] Hesiod: *Theogony*, 116, πρώτιστα χάος γένετ᾽, αὐτὰρ ἔπειτα Γαῖ᾽ εὐρύστερνος.

[21] *E. g.*, Rabast, *op. cit.*, "Die Erschaffung eines Chaos ist ein Widerspruch in sich selbst und passt nicht zu dem Gott des Kosmos und könnte höchstens von dem Fürsten der Finsternis stammen".

[22] Merrill F. Unger: *op. cit.*, pp. 27–35; Arno C. Gaebelein: *The Annotated Bible*, Vol. 1, 1913, p. 16, "It is of the greatest importance to understand that the condition in which the earth (not the heavens) is described in the second verse is not how God created it in the beginning"; G. H. Pember: *Earth's Earliest Ages*, n. d., pp. 26 ff.; *The Scofield Reference Bible*, 1945, p. 3; *The Pilgrim Bible*, 1948, p. 1.

[23] Isaiah 45:18 is often treated as though it taught that God did not create the earth as a תֹהוּ. This is a misinterpretation. The prophet is simply stating the purpose of creation. It should be noted that this very chapter of Isaiah (v. 11) speaks of God as "forming darkness" יֹצֵר חֹשֶׁךְ.

[24] The LXX (Codex B) renders ἡ δὲ γῆ ἦν ἀόρατος καὶ ἀκατασκεύαστος. The Vulgate, Terra autem erat inanis et vacua.

same meaning as תֹהוּ, namely, "empty", "void", "waste".
The earth, therefore, is described as a desolation and a waste.
This does not affirm that it was a confused mass, in the sense
of being disordered or jumbled, but simply that it was not
habitable, not ready for man. The same condition was also
present at the close of the first day, except that at that time
light had also been brought into existence. In so far as the
words תֹהוּ וָבֹהוּ are concerned we must conclude that they
simply describe the earth as not habitable. There is no reason
why God might not have pronounced the condition set forth
by the first circumstantial clause of verse two as "good".

The second clause affirms that darkness was upon the face
of the abyss, *i. e.*, the primeval waters, and the third clause
declares that the Spirit of God was brooding upon the waters.
Is this a description of a chaotic condition, a condition in
which everything has become topsy-turvy as the result of a
judgment? To ask that question is to answer it. Despite all
that has been said to the contrary, we would affirm that verse
two describes a condition of things in which all was under
the control of the Spirit of God.

It is true that man could not at that time have lived upon
the earth, but, for that matter the earth was not ready for
man until the sixth day. At the same time even though the
earth was not in a habitable condition, it was as God desired
it to be. It stands out in great contrast to the finished world
of verse thirty-one, but at every stage in the development
God is in control, things are as he desires them to be.

It would probably be wise to abandon the term "chaos"
as a designation of the conditions set forth in verse two. The
three-fold statement of circumstances in itself seems to imply
order. The material of which this earth consists was at that
time covered with water, and darkness was all about. Over
the waters, however, brooded God's Spirit.[25] There is something of the awesome in the description. But things were not
always to continue so. It was God's purpose to change this
primeval condition. He would introduce light, would divide
the waters, bring forth the dry land, make the heavenly bodies,

---

[25] Without at this point seeking to defend the position, I would affirm
that רוּחַ אֱלֹהִים is to be translated "Spirit of God".

fill the earth with animals and finally place upon it man. There is majesty in the first chapter of Genesis, but that majesty is greatly impaired when the first three verses are misinterpreted.

CONCLUSION

By way of conclusion we would affirm that the first verse serves as a broad, comprehensive statement of the fact of creation. Verse two describes the earth as it came from the hands of the Creator and as it existed at the time when God commanded the light to shine forth. The first recorded step in the process of fashioning the earth into the form in which it now appears was God's remarkable utterance, "Let there be light".

THE INTERPRETATION OF GENESIS 1:2

EDWARD J. YOUNG

IN THE recent interest devoted to mythology and its relation to the Bible the first chapter of Genesis has not been neglected.[1] In particular the second verse has received considerable attention. It will be our purpose in this article to ascertain what relationship, if any, the second verse of Genesis sustains to mythology and also to present a positive interpretation and explanation of the verse.

Recent Studies of Genesis 1:2

That we may arrive at the correct interpretation of Genesis 1:2 it will be well first of all to consider certain recent expositions in which attention is paid to mythology and its supposed relationship to the verse. As an introduction to the subject we may consider the remarks of Rabast.

Karlheinz Rabast, whose recent death is a severe blow to biblical scholarship, was a pastor at the Martin Luther Church in Dresden and the author of an excellent commentary on the first eleven chapters of Genesis. He wrote as a Bible believer, and rejected the documentary hypothesis in a very clear cut and decisive fashion.[2] His work is filled with useful comments and he makes genuinely significant and useful contributions to the interpretation of the early chapters of Genesis.

Rabast rejects the "Restitution Hypothesis" which would posit a long interval of time between verses one and two, giving as his reason that it is unlikely that the Scripture would pass over such a great catastrophe in silence when it mentions in this context many comparatively less important

---

[1] *Cf.* Brevard S. Childs: *Myth and Reality in the Old Testament*, 1960. This work gives a good bibliography. Attention may also be directed to the informative article by Lester Wikström: "Till frågan om begreppet myt" in *Svensk Exegetisk Årsbok*, XVI, 1952, pp. 66–80.

[2] Karlheinz Rabast: *Die Genesis*, 1951, pp. 15–29.

16

matters.[3] According to Rabast, verse two does not describe
any original or chaotic or raw material of the earth, but rather
presents a background without existence, the indescribable
Nothing. Nothing, however, asserts Rabast, cannot be described in words. In other, therefore, to describe this Nothing,
the writer of Genesis used old mythological formulations and
expressions. Indeed, the verse itself may be characterized as
a veritable mythological treasure house.[4] According to differ-
ing conceptions of ancient mythology the world arose from a
waste and desolation or from an original sea or from darkness
or from an original egg. In Genesis these primitive and often
conflicting representations could be employed because they no
longer possessed their mythological character. We need not
endeavor, therefore, to demythologize the Bible, because the
Bible has already been demythologized. Here in the second
verse of Genesis are fragments of a foreign world-view which
now serve a greater concept than ever before. They serve to
describe the existence-less Nothing from which God forms his
creation.[5] Rabast, therefore, would paraphrase the thought of
the second verse as follows: "In the beginning was Nothing,
and over this Nothing hovered the Spirit of God. The cosmos
did not arise from a chaos, but from a Nothing . . . . Nothing,
however, cannot come from nothing, unless there is a miracle,
and it is this miracle of creation which is set forth here."[6]

"Für diese theosophische Erweiterung liegt aber kein Grund vor, und
es ist von vornherein unwahrscheinlich, dass eine so wichtige und
wesentliche Tatsache gleichsam zwischen den Zeilen stehen sollte, während
andere verhältnismässig nebensächliche Dinge in demselben Zusammen-
hang breit und ausführlich geschildert werden" (op. cit., p. 46).

[4] The phrase "eine wahre mythologische Schatzkammer" appears in
Gunkel's commentary (p. 103) where it is attributed to Schwally, Archiv
für Religionswissenschaft, IX, 169. I have not seen this last mentioned work.

[5] "Um dieses Nichts zu beschreiben, werden alte mythologische Formu-
lierungen und Ausdrücke verwendet" (op. cit., p. 46). Rabast quotes a
passage from Zimmerli in which the latter seeks to show that, just as an
Arabian construction in Palmyra has used Roman pillars and the El
Azhar mosque in Cairo whole rows of Roman columns, so in Genesis 1:2
fragments of a foreign world-view have been incorporated. The passage is
from Walther Zimmerli: Die Urgeschichte, Zürich, 1943.

[6] "Am Anfang war ein Nichts, und über diesem Nichts schwebte der
Geist Gottes. Nicht aus einem Chaos entstand der Kosmos, sondern aus

It is a miracle which God alone can perform, and this he does through his Word.

In his interpretation of verse two Rabast is not alone among modern scholars. Nevertheless, there are serious objections to his view, and these must be considered. In passing we may note a logical inconsistency in Rabast's presentation of the argument. If it is true, as he asserts, that the Nothing is indescribable and cannot be described in words, then it is passing strange that verse two is thought to be a description of Nothing. This is irrationalism such as characterizes much recent discussion of the early chapters of Genesis.

It is also well to ask why the mention of ancient mythological elements should be considered a description of Nothing. Some of these elements are found in the Babylonian account of creation, the so-called "Enuma Elish", and there is no evidence that in that document they are intended to describe or portray Nothing. In fact, what characterizes this work is that it does not present a true doctrine of creatio *ex nihilo*, but rather begins with the assumption that matter is already at hand. It is true that Enuma Elish posits a time when heaven and earth had not been formed, but when Tiamat, Mummu and Apsu existed together, apparently without any beginning. Furthermore there also appears a fatalism to which all, gods and men alike, are subject. Whatever may be said about the Enuma Elish, it is certain that no doctrine of absolute creation is to be found in it, and no attempt to describe a Nothing.[7] If then, in the sources in which these ancient mythological elements are originally found there is no

---

dem Nichts! . . . Aus einem Nichts kann aber nichts werden, oder es muss ein Wunder geschehen, und um dieses Wunder der Schöpfung handelt es sich hier" (*op. cit.*, p. 47).

[7] As an introduction to the study of the Babylonian creation account, see Anton Deimel S. I.: *"Enuma Eliš" und Hexaëmeron*, Rome, 1934. His comment at this point is pertinent, "Erst nachdem die beiden Urprinzipien *Abzu-Tiamat* von ihren Söhnen getötet sind, können ihre Kadaver, aus deren Bestandteilen die Welt von den beiden Weltbaumeistern umgeformt wird, als 'Chaos' aufgefasst werden. Hier ist aber zu beachten, dass wir ohne die klare Stelle der hl. Schrift und anderer ausserbabylonischer Quellen wohl kaum je auf den Gedanken gekommen wären, in den Kadavern von *Abzu-Tiamat* Personifikationen des 'Weltchaos' zu suchen" (p. 84).

connection with Nothing, what warrant have we for assuming that when they are combined in Genesis they describe Nothing?

Again, had it been the intention of the writer to use verse two for the purpose suggested by Rabast, we should have expected some indication of that purpose. If Moses had intended to describe Nothing, why did he not use language more suitable for his task? Why, instead, does he in so emphatic a manner immediately draw attention to the earth? It is not Nothing which forms the subject matter of the second verse, but the earth. All the language of this verse is suitable to describe the earth, but not the "indescribable" Nothing. If Moses had intended to do what Rabast claims, we should have expected some indication of that fact.

The language of Genesis 1:2 is for the most part found elsewhere in the Bible in passages where its meaning is perfectly clear. And in these other passages the words are not used to describe Nothing. This becomes apparent from a consideration of Isaiah 45:18 in which passage the purpose of creating the world is given. According to Isaiah 45:18, God did not create the world to be a desolation or an uninhabitable place, but to be inhabited. The meaning is not, "God did not create the world to be a Nothing". Isaiah does not make a disjunction between Nothing on the one hand and an inhabitable world on the other. In this passage the word תהו is obviously a description of the world after it has been created. To be a desolation, however, was not the purpose for which God created it. Isaiah does not mean that after its creation the world was a Nothing. And inasmuch as such a meaning is impossible in Isaiah 45:18, it is likewise impossible in Genesis 1:2, which also refers to an earth that has already been created.

Perhaps the most significant interpretation of Genesis to appear in recent years is found in the work of Gerhard von Rad. Von Rad holds that the first chapter of Genesis contains the essence of priestly knowledge in concentrated form. It is doctrine which has grown up and become enriched over many long years, and it is precisely well measured and carefully thought out. It is to be taken exactly as it stands.[8]

[8] "Diese Sätze sind theologisch nicht leicht zu überinterpretieren!" (Gerhard von Rad: *Das erste Buch Mose*, 1952, p. 36).

The first of the theological specifications with which we have to deal, says von Rad, is the statement about the original chaotic condition of the earth. The priestly writing comes to this subject with a row of concepts that were familiar to it. One of these is the phrase רוּחַ אֱלֹהִים which von Rad renders, "Gottessturm", *i. e.*, a fearful storm. This expression in particular, he thinks, belongs to the description of the chaotic and does not yet lead to the thought of creation, inasmuch as in the following context no result is attributed to the action expressed by the participle.[9]

In our text, so the argument continues, the actual mythical meaning has been completely lost. Hence, we must even reject the assumption that in order to make clearer the chaotic condition of the original material the priestly writing had to employ foreign and half-mythological conceptions. These expressions have long since lost their mythical character and have become stereotyped. Von Rad rightly rejects the view of the relationship between Genesis one and the Babylonian accounts which characterized the advocates of the "Babel-Bibel" controversy.

Verse two, therefore, according to von Rad, speaks not only of a condition which was actually present in the beginning of time, but it also points to a possibility that might recur. Behind the creation of all things lies the abyss of formlessness, and into this abyss all that is created stands ready again to fall. It is belief in the doctrine of creation which must prevent

---

[9] Von Rad appeals to Daniel 7:2 in support of his interpretation. But this appeal is not justifiable. In Daniel the sea is introduced symbolically in a vision which is not the case in Genesis. The sea in Daniel (יַמָּא and not תְּהוֹם) is a symbol of the earth or mankind (Dan. 7:17). The winds are the four cardinal winds, which God employs to stir up humanity. In other words the events which occur upon this earth are the result of the working of heavenly forces. In Daniel the winds burst forth upon the great sea; they do not merely blow over it. Vergil's well known lines illustrate the same thing that is found in Daniel

> . . . ac venti, velut agmine facto,
> qua data porta, ruunt et terras turbine perflant.
> incubuere mari totumque a sedibus imis
> una Eurusque Notusque ruunt creberque procellis
> Africus et vastos volvunt ad litora fluctus (*Aeneid*, 1:82 ff.).

There is nothing in Genesis 1:2 comparable to this "breaking forth" of the winds (*cf.* Young: *The Prophecy of Daniel*, Grand Rapids, 1957).

20

man from falling back again.[10] The polarity which is expressed in the first chapter is therefore not that of nothing as over against creation, but rather that of chaos and cosmos. The thought of creation from nothing is found in verse one, but the remainder of the chapter stresses the contrast between formlessness or chaos and the completed, well-ordered universe, the cosmos. Hence, concludes von Rad, there is good reason for verse one preceding verse two.

Karl Barth also has written in recent times on the second verse of Genesis.[11] Does this verse, he asks, speak of the *informitas materiae*, the *rudis indigestaque moles* as an actual (whether founded in itself or willed and established by God), original and raw condition of the world? If that is the case, he argues, there is a dilemma, for if the condition described in verse two is not an independent existence apart from God, it must be God's creation. If, on the other hand, it is not God's creation, it must be an actuality independent of God and his work. If, however, neither of these is correct there is no dilemma, and there is a third way out.[12] Before proceeding, however, to give this third position Barth makes a few remarks about the nature of verse two. He agrees with Gunkel that the verse describes the chaos, which is out of accord with what was stated in the first verse, and also with what follows.[13]

[10] "Dass hinter allem Geschaffenen der Abgrund der Gestaltlosigkeit liegt, dass ferner alles Geschaffene ständig bereit ist, im Abgrund des Gestaltlosen zu versinken, dass also das Chaotische schlechthin die Bedrohung alles Geschaffenen bedeutet, das ist eine Urerfahrung des Menschen und eine ständige Anfechtung seines Glaubens. An ihr musste sich der Schöpfungsglaube bewähren" (von Rad: *op. cit.*, p. 38). This consideration is not derived from the text by exegesis. In the first chapter of Genesis there is not the slightest hint of the possibility of a return to "chaos" anymore than of a return, for example, to the condition of "the third day".

[11] *Die Kirchliche Dogmatik*, III/1 *Die Lehre von der Schöpfung*, Zollikon-Zürich, 1945, pp. 111–121.

[12] "Aber eben das ist die Frage, ob v 2 von der *informitas materiae*, von der *rudis indigestaque moles* tatsächlich als von einem (sei es in sich selbst begründeten, sei es von Gott gewollten und gesetzten) *wirklichen* (im Sinn der nach v 3 f. geschaffenen Dinge 'wirklich' zu nennenden) Ur- und Rohzustand der Welt geredet wird. Nur wenn das der Fall ist, besteht jenes Dilemma. Wenn das nicht der Fall ist, dann besteht jenes Dilemma nur scheinbar, dann gibt es hier tatsächlich ein Drittes" (*op. cit.*, p. 114).

[13] *Op. cit.*, p. 114. Barth thinks that the words תֹהוּ וָבֹהוּ could have had

Hence, the writer could only oppose it and interpret it *in malam partem.*

With respect to the dilemma, Barth asserts that we are not compelled either to accept the one position or the other. There is no talk here, he thinks, about an original, raw condition of the earth, only the original and raw condition of the evil, of sin, apostasy and all its results. There is thought of the possibility which God, as he comes to creation, passes by, just as a human creator in choosing one particular work, rejects others, leaving them unfulfilled behind him. Verse three, in which God speaks, shows that the work which he chooses is that of the heaven and the earth. Verse two, on the other hand, sets forth a condition of the world about which God's Word has not spoken; it is a condition that does without the Word of God. The verse speaks of the Nothing, which is rendered nothing by God's act of creation. The Spirit of God, a divine power, cannot make good this loss, for it is not

---

no positive meaning for the Israelitish-Jewish language and reflection, but were merely personifications of the abominable. "Die Erde als *tohu* und *bohu* ist die Erde, die als solche *nichts* ist, die ihren Schöpfer verhöhnt und die auch für den Himmel über ihr nur eine Beleidigung, eine Bedrohung mit derselben Nichtigkeit sein kann" (*op. cit.,* p. 115). תְּהוֹם, because it is indefinite, and used as a proper name, reminds us that originally it designated a mythical, personified being. Barth thinks that in formal connection with the Babylonian tradition the element of water is treated as the principle which is absolutely opposed to the creation of God in its abundance and despotism (*op. cit.,* p. 115). Where the biblical evidence for such a statement occurs, I do not know. From this original flood, thinks Barth, nothing can nor will become good (p. 116).

The darkness is taken by Barth as that in which there is no recognition nor objectivity. It can in no sense be regarded as also a potentially positive substance (p. 117). Nothing good can come out of darkness. It should be noted, however, in opposition to what Barth writes, that God gives a name to the darkness, just as he does to the light. Both are therefore good and well-pleasing to him; both are created, although the express creation of the darkness, as of other objects in verse two, is not stated, and both serve his purpose of forming the day.

Barth rightly rejects the interpretation of רוּחַ as "wind", and thinks that the representation is that of a hovering bird moving its wings, and that this bird will brood. Hence, we are close to the old picture of a world-egg (*op. cit.,* p. 118). This spirit belongs to the essence and character of the world of abomination (Greuelwelt), which would have condemned the spirit to the weakness of a hovering or brooding bird. This passive, contemplative role is not that of the true God (*op. cit.,* p. 119).

God's Word, but can only bring the loss more glaringly into the light.[14]

Without God's Word, says Barth, the world does not have existence nor essentiality nor the goodness of the creature which is later described as the creature of the Word of God and so the true creature. What is left to us in verse two is a picture of the world, negated and rejected, passed over and left behind. Because this world in its absurd manner is completely different from the world willed and created by God, because it is actual as the world of the non-existing, the essenceless, the through and through non-good, because it was only too well known to the writer and to the whole biblical witness as the shadow, which as a matter of fact rests on the willed and created world of God, it is here mentioned. What is described in verse two is not the original, raw condition but the past of the actual cosmos which was created by God's Word.[15] It is thus described as obsolete, for God has passed it by. Only the shadow of this *hayetha* (*i. e.*, the earth was) can lie on the cosmos which was really created by God. And this shadow can only exist when God's Word and the actual choice and actual work of God, and so the actuality of the cosmos itself, are forgotten. In loving what God hates, the creature can bring back this previous condition. When men do this God, on his part, can repent of having created them and bring about the flood. This is so, because the creature in his differentiation from God is not Against God but Non-God. By misusing his freedom man can look back and bring back the past, so that that past can become a present and a future to what it opposes. That is the risk which God has taken upon himself in the venture of creation. Genesis 1:2 speaks from the "Old", that according to II Corinthians 5:17 has passed away radically in the death and resurrection of Jesus Christ. It says that the chaos, looked at not from the new but from the old creation, is really the old, passed-by existence of this world.[16]

---

[14] Barth describes the Spirit as "eine göttliche Kraft, die nun doch gerade nicht die des schöpferischen Wortes ist, kann diesen Mangel nicht gut machen, kann ihn vielmehr nur noch greller ins Licht stellen" (*op. cit.*, p. 119).

[15] In this paragraph I have sought to give a summary of Barth's thought as it is expressed in *op. cit.*, pp. 119 f.

[16] This is a brief summary of Barth's comments (*op. cit.*, pp. 120 f.).

It would appear that there are certain similarities between the position of Rabast and that of Barth. Both in their interpretations have quite evidently been somewhat influenced by Zimmerli.[17] Both hold that the second verse of Genesis is a description of Nothing. At this point, however, the similarity really ceases. Rabast comes to this interpretation upon exegetical grounds. He believes that the writer, by means of his use of old mythological expressions, really intended to set forth a description of Nothing. With this conclusion the present writer is unable to agree. He has already set forth certain objections to it. At the same time it must be acknowledged that Rabast has intended to do full justice to proper exegesis in arriving at his conclusion. On the basis of what may legitimately be called exegetical considerations he arrives at the position which he adopts. That position, we think, is erroneous, but we do acknowledge that Rabast has sought to follow an exegetical procedure.

With Barth, however, the case is quite different. With Barth, at least as far as the consideration of Genesis 1:2 is concerned, exegesis plays quite a minor role. It is true that Barth does engage in exegetical procedure (see his discussion on pp. 114–119 — by far the most valuable part of his treatment). Had he done only this, we would have no quarrel with his procedure. But he does far more. Having once exegetically established a meaning for his text, Barth now proceeds to impose upon that text an interpretation which is wholly foreign to the Bible.

We may perhaps, to a point, understand this interpretation if we note that Barth holds that the creation is *Geschichte* but not historical *Geschichte*.[18] History, says Barth, is objec-

---

[17] It would seem that Barth has also been deeply influenced by Gunkel. Barth's views cannot be derived from the text as it stands. Gunkel's divisive criticism, however, seems to make room for an exposition such as that of Barth. Gunkel writes, "Vielmehr ist zuzugeben, dass hier ein innerer Widerspruch vorliegt, der aber *geschichtlich* zu verstehen ist: der Stoff von v. 2 gehört zu den vom Judentum vorgefundenen Elementen, v. 1 ist vom Judentum selbst hinzugefügt. Dass P eine solche Schilderung des Chaos aufnehmen konnte, zeigt, dass auch er den Gedanken einer creatio ex nihilo (II Mak 7[28] Hbr 11[3]) noch nicht deutlich erfasst hatte" (*Die Genesis*, Göttingen, 1922, p. 103).

[18] Note particularly the following statement: "Die ganze Geschichte ohne Ausnahme ist insofern immer auch unhistorisch, von der ganzen

tive, because accessible and perceivable by men. But the creation is not history and no history of it can be given ("und kann es von ihr auch keine Historie geben", *op. cit.*, p. 84). It can therefore only be unhistorical *Geschichte* and only unhistorical history writing (*Geschichtsschreibung*) can deal with it.

It will not be our purpose to attempt an exposition of Barth's usage of the terms *Geschichte* and *Historie*. What it is precisely that Barth has in mind by the term *Geschichte* is difficult to determine. It is not so difficult, however, to discover what he does not have in mind by that term. It would seem that when Barth places the creation account in the realm of *Geschichte* he is in actual fact denying that Genesis one is a reliable and factual account of what actually transpired.

It may not be out of place at this juncture to ask what history is. In answering the question we would hold that history does, of course, include the study of matters accessible to the human mind for investigation, but it may also include matters which the unaided human mind cannot investigate, but concerning which God has revealed information. Unaided, for example, the human mind cannot study the creation, but it is legitimate to hold that God can reveal certain information about the creation. Man can study this information and upon the basis of his study can make true statements concerning the creation. The study of this revealed material is as truly the study of history as is the study of Caesar's accounts of ancient Gaul. We may, therefore, indeed, we must, approach the first chapter of Genesis as a reliable historical document, trustworthy in all its statements because its contents have been communicated to us by God.[19]

It goes without saying that, unaided, Moses could not have made an investigation of the creation and come to the con-

---

Geschichte kann insofern immer nur unhistorisch berichtet werden, als in der ganzen Geschichte Gottes Schöpfung weitergeht, als die ganze Geschichte in allen ihren Bewegungen, Verhältnissen und Gestalten immer auch eine Komponente hat, in der sie unmittelbar zu Gott, in der sie unmittelbare göttliche Setzung ist" (*op. cit.*, pp. 84 f.). For an exposition of the underlying philosophy *cf.* C. Van Til: *The New Modernism*, Philadelphia, 1946.

[19] The defense of this position will be found in *Thy Word Is Truth*, Grand Rapids, 1957.

clusion that the events which he related in Genesis one actually happened as they are there recorded.[20] But does it follow that God himself could not have revealed to Moses those events, and that God's Spirit could not have superintended the recording of those events so that the final written product was an accurate account of what had actually transpired? Barth says not a word about this possibility, for were he to do so, he would have to reject the idea that the creation account is *Geschichte* and not *Historie*. Granted that man, inasmuch as he is himself something created, could not have investigated the creation on his own, we may nevertheless assert that God revealed the account to Moses who wrote it down. The account, there, is historical. The study of history is simply the study of those things which have actually taken place, whether the historian has come to their knowledge by means of his own investigation or whether information concerning them has been revealed by almighty God.

It is this point which we must remember when discussing Barth's interpretation. By his usage of the word *Geschichte*, does Barth intend us to understand that the events recorded in the first chapter of the Bible actually took place as Scripture asserts that they did? This question, we believe, must be answered in the negative.[21] What Barth writes is not partic-

[20] The Mosaic authorship of Genesis is herein assumed. It is an assumption supported by Scripture and best explains the many problems involved in the question of the authorship of Genesis. It does not preclude the possibility that, in writing Genesis, Moses may have employed previously existing documents. For a cogent defense of Mosaic authorship cf. Oswald T. Allis: *The Five Books of Moses*, Philadelphia, 1949.

[21] Barth remarks explicitly, "entzieht sich ihre geschichtliche Wirklichkeit aller historischen Beobachtung und Berichterstattung und kann sie auch in den biblischen Schöpfungsgeschichten nur in Form reiner Sage bezeugt werden" (*op. cit.*, p. 44). This is to deny genuine special revelation. Why cannot the all-powerful God communicate truth in propositional form to man concerning the creation? If he cannot do this, he is not all-powerful, not the God of Scripture. Barth really makes God to be limited by man. From the fact that creation is not historically observable by man it does not follow that God is limited to witnessing to the creation only in pure saga. Again, "Die biblische *Schöpfungsgeschichte* aber ist, entsprechend dem singulären Charakter ihres Gegenstandes, *reine* Sage, so wie es — beides als Ausnahme von der Regel — an anderen Stellen der Bibel auch reine und als solche kaum ernstlich anzufechtende Historie gibt" (*op. cit.*, p. 89).

ularly easy to follow, but there seems to be no evidence that he regards the events recorded in Genesis one as actually having occurred. These events, consequently, are not historical. To assign them to a realm labelled *Geschichte*, is in reality to deny that they ever took place. What Barth discusses in his comments on Genesis 1:2 is not the condition of the physical earth as it actually was at a certain time. What Barth does, it would seem, is to take the language of Genesis 1:2 and use it as a vehicle for the expression of certain ideas. His remarks are to be understood upon the basis of a particular philosophical background.

Was there ever a time, it is pertinent to ask, when this particular earth on which we live was in precisely that condition described in Genesis 1:2? That question Barth would probably regard as irrelevant.[22] His interest lies elsewhere. Indeed, we have mentioned Barth's comments on Genesis not because they have made a contribution to exegesis or to the genuine elucidation of the text, but merely because they are in the forefront of discussion at the present time.

In the works considered thus far there has been an emphasis upon the point of view that mythological elements are to be found in Genesis 1:2. In what manner, however, are we to interpret these supposed elements? Have we really arrived at a solution when we merely assert that the writer employed as much mythological material as suited his purpose but that he actually rejected its original significance? Is there not a better way of approaching the subject, one that is more truly Scriptural?

Moses and Mythology

If we come to the Bible with the presupposition that it is the trustworthy Word of God, we shall be inclined to take seriously what the Bible itself has to say about the entire account of creation. May it not be that God spoke to Adam

[22] "Und nun sind wir doch wohl in der Lage, auf jenes Dilemma: ob in v 2 von einem in sich selbst begründeten oder von einem von Gott gewollten und gesetzten Ur- und Rohzustand der Welt die Rede sei? einergemassen belehrt zurückzublicken. Wir antworten: weder von Einen noch vom Anderen!" (*op. cit.*, p. 119).

concerning the creation and that Adam taught the revealed truth on this subject to his children? With the entrance of sin into the world the human race became divided. There was the line of Seth, the line of promise, and there was also the line of Cain. Among the Sethites the truth would have been handed down from generation to generation. The same would probably be true among the Cainites. Oral transmission however, is no guarantee of accurate transmittal. Even among the promised line, there would be the danger of corruption unless the tradition was somehow preserved and protected. Even in the line of promise there was the danger that the truth might be perverted and in time even become unrecognizable. It was necessary that the truth concerning creation should be written down that the church might possess that truth in an uncorrupted form.

The man whom God chose to perform this task was, we believe, Moses. But how did Moses learn the truth which he expressed in Genesis one? Obviously he could not have learned it first-hand. But there were other means of learning this truth. It may be that Moses had access to written documents which were at his disposal. It may also be that he was acquainted with oral tradition. If, however, we approach this question Scripturally we will be compelled to the conclusion that the author of Genesis one was a holy man who was borne by the Holy Spirit. That is to say, God, in his providence, prepared by training and education the particular man whom he desired to write the first chapter of the Bible, and when that man set to the work of writing he was superintended by the Spirit of God with the result that what he wrote was what the Spirit of God desired him to write. If he did employ ancient documents he was protected and guided in his use of them so that he chose from them only what God desired him to employ. In this process of writing, he was no mere automaton, but a responsible writer. Although superintended by the Spirit, he used his own judgment and made a genuine choice and selection of material. The resultant writing, therefore, was Scripture, trustworthy Scripture, indeed, infallible Scripture. It is this answer to which we must come if we permit ourselves to be guided by what the Bible has to say concerning itself.

Indeed, it is only on the basis of the Christian theism presented in the Bible that the whole question of the authorship of Genesis one can have validity. If we reject the explicit testimony of the Bible to itself we are left to the free play of our imagination. We may then toy with invalid and irrational ideas such as the one that is so widespread today, namely, that it is impossible to express creation in words but only in terms of myth. But in dallying with such thoughts we are removing ourselves from the truth.

The facts of creation, we have suggested, were probably handed down from father to son. And if among the promised line error may soon have been fused with truth before the truth was finally preserved through inscripturation, what may we say of the line of Cain? Certainly in this line error would have had free play. Superstition would soon have entered in and obscured the truth. This is the reason why among many peoples we find accounts of creation bearing some relation to what is recorded in Genesis one. Among the various nations and peoples of earth the truth would indeed have been handed down, but it would have been a grossly garbled truth, one encrusted with layers of superstition. Hence, in almost all cosmogonies there are certain elements of truth itself, namely, the formal resemblances which these cosmogonies sustain to the contents of Genesis one.

How did Moses employ the material which was at his disposal? Did he find readily available mythological sources upon which he could draw as he desired? Let us consider this question more precisely with respect to Genesis 1:2. When he wished to make reference to the abyss, he employed the word תְּהוֹם. Indeed, it is difficult to see what other word he could have used. At the same time, he may have been conscious that this word, at least in its sound, bore a resemblance to the name of the goddess of the Babylonian epic. He used the word, however, in such a way that it was free of any mythological connotations which it might have borne elsewhere in the ancient world. He made it serve to bring to the reader's mind the great deep or ocean, and this he did in such a way as to exclude from the reader's mind any thought of superstition or polytheism. In so employing the word, was Moses consciously rejecting mythology? Possibly so, but possibly he was not even thinking of mythology. He may have been merely employing the one word in the language which best expressed his thought, irrespective of whether that word might have had different connotations for other peoples. It is not difficult to ascertain what Moses meant by the word. His writing makes it clear that the תְהוֹם is not a goddess. Whatever connotations the word may have summoned before the minds of others, as Moses employs it in Genesis it indicates the abyss or the great ocean.

The same might be said for each of the words and phrases found in the verse. They are not necessarily demythologized words or phrases, but are clear-cut Hebrew words which express the positive thought that there was a time when man could not live upon the earth. Other peoples and other nations may have used these same words, or at least words that were somewhat similar to them, for the purpose of expressing myths or grotesque cosmogonies. With Moses, however, these words have long since lost whatever such associations they might have had with the peoples of other nations. This is not to say that they represent Moses' conscious rejection of mythology; it is merely to say that they were current in Hebrew and were suitable for Moses' purposes.

We may compare our modern usage of the names of the days of the week. When we speak of Wednesday or Thursday, for example, we are not consciously rejecting an old mythology. We do not consciously think of Wodan's day or Thor's day. Whatever old mythological connotations may have once adhered to these words are long since forgotten. In the course of time mere habit and custom may have led to the inclusion of these words in the language. If, therefore, some two or three thousand years from now an historian should assert that the usage of these names of the days of the week in the English language represented our antipathy to mythology, he would be in error. It would not even be correct to assert that we knew the existence of the old Norse mythology and consciously rejected it, for many modern users of the names of the weekdays have no idea of the original meaning of those names.

May not the same have been true in the case of Moses? May he not have used the vocabulary that was at his disposal

30

and was best adapted to express the truth he wished to set forth? We are not really warranted in speaking of Genesis 1:2 as a treasure house of mythological expressions any more than we are warranted in speaking of the names of the days of the week in English as a group of mythological expressions. What Moses has written does not reveal in any particularly clear manner a rejection of ancient mythology, but it does state what Moses wished it to state, namely, the condition in which this earth existed until God uttered the command that light should spring into existence.

The Meaning of Genesis 1:2

Attention is immediately directed to the earth.[23] It is true that the second verse of Genesis does not represent a continuation of the narrative of verse one, but, as it were, a new beginning.[24] Grammatically, it is not to be construed with

[23] וְהָאָרֶץ. The emphasis is retained by LXX ἡ δε γῆ, and the Vulgate, terra autem. To maintain this emphasis in the English versions is difficult. King James renders "And the earth" which is weak. To preserve the emphasis we should probably render "Now the earth" or "The earth moreover". König (Die Genesis, Gutersloh, 1925, p. 141) brings out the emphasis, "Und die Erde ihrerseits". So Aalders (Het Boek Genesis, Eerste Deel (Korte Verklaring der Heilige Schrift), Kampen, 1949, p. 78), "Met nadruk wordt het woord ‚aarde' vooropgezet: wat nu de aarde betreft, deze was ‚enkel ledigheid en vormeloosheid en duisternis over een vloed' ".

[24] I have defended this point of view in "The Relation of the First Verse of Genesis One to Verses Two and Three" in Westminster Theological Journal, Vol. XXI, No. 2 (May 1959), pp. 133–146. It is also supported by Otto Procksch, Die Genesis, Leipzig, 1913, "v. 2 schliesst inhaltlich nicht als Fortsetzung an v. 1, sondern beginnt ganz neu. Der zuständliche Nominalsatz findet seinen Hauptsatz in v. 3" (p. 425); Karlheinz Rabast, op. cit., p. 46, "V. 2 ff. ist nicht die logische Fortsetzung von V. 1. Das ganze Kapitel könnte ohne weiteres erst mit V. 2 beginnen, und umgekehrt müssten wir uns auch mit V. 1 begnügen lassen. Der Sinnzusammenhang von V. 1 und 2 ist wohl nur so zu verstehen, dass V. 1 die Überschrift ist, und alles Folgende ist Entfaltung dieser Überschrift"; Helmuth Frey: Das Buch der Anfänge Kapitel 1–11 des ersten Buches Mose, Calwer Verlag, Stuttgart, 1953, "Mit V. 2 beginnt nicht die Fortsetzung, sondern die Ausführung des Themas, das in der Überschrift angegeben wurde" (p. 14); von Rad, (op. cit., p. 37), "Diesen V. 1 wird man als die summarische Aussage dessen, was im Folgenden schrittweise entfaltet wird, verstehen

the preceding, but with what follows. Nevertheless, by its
introductory words, "and the earth", it does take up the
thought of the first verse. It does this, however, by way of
exclusion. No longer is our thought to rest upon the heaven
and the earth, the entirety of created phenomena, but merely
upon the earth. The word הָאָרֶץ stands first for the sake of emphasis. It is
the subject to which attention must be directed, and it is the
grand theme, not merely of the remainder of the chapter, but
of the remainder of the Bible itself. It is this earth on which
we live with which the Scripture has to do and to which it will
direct its thought.[25] Thus, from a contemplation of the entire

---

dürfen". The same position is presupposed, although not explicitly stated,
in the exegesis of Keil and Delitzsch (*Biblical Commentary on the Old
Testament*, Vol. I, 1949, pp. 47 f.).

It is essentially this position which is adopted by Ridderbos: "Genesis i 1
und 2" in *Oudtestamentische Studiën*, Deel XII, *Studies on the Book of
Genesis*, 1958, p. 231: "In Vers 2 wird beschrieben, wie der Zustand der
Welt war, bevor Gott mit seinem ‚Sprechen' begann. Und um nun den
Eindruck wegzunehmen, als ob die Erde in ihrem Wüstsein und ihrer
Leere eine selbständige Grösse neben oder gegenüber Gott darstelle, . . .
lässt der Autor an dem Ausspruch von Vers 2 noch den von Vers 1 voran-
gehen." Ridderbos does, however, seek to express a connection in thought
between vv. 1 and 2, namely, "And it came about that the earth was at
first, etc." („Und [dabei ging es wie folgt zu:] die Erde war [anfänglich]
wüst und leer usw."). While this seems to me to be a correct interpretation, nevertheless it does add to the language of Genesis 1:2a, which is a
mere circumstantial clause, as Ridderbos also acknowledges. Delitzsch
(*A New Commentary on Genesis*, Vol. I, New York, 1889, p. 77) comments,
"It is within the all-embracing work of creation, stated in ver. 1, that ver. 2
takes up its position, at the point when the creation of this earth and its
heaven begins". On the other hand Simpson ("Genesis" in *The Interpreter's
Bible*, Vol. I, 1952, p. 467) thinks that verse two is an intrusion into the
narrative as it left the hand of P, and that it was probably added to supply
a seeming lack in P, namely, a reference to the primeval chaos. If this
were actually the case there would seem to be little point in endeavoring
seriously to ascertain the precise relationship between verses one and two,
inasmuch as verse two would not be an integral part of the original
narrative.

[25] Keil's words are to the point: "Though treating of the creation of the
heaven and the earth, the writer, both here and in what follows, describes
with minuteness the original condition and progressive formation of the
earth alone, and says nothing more respecting the heaven than is actually
requisite in order to show its connection with the earth. He is writing for

universe, or, we may more accurately say, of all created worlds
and bodies besides our own, the Bible turns to a geocentric
emphasis,[26] and it maintains that geocentric emphasis throughout to its last page. This is not to say that the Bible now
entertains an incorrect view of the relationship of the heavenly
bodies, positing the earth as the physical center of the universe.
On that subject the Bible really does not speak. It is merely
that attention is focused upon this world on which we live,
upon which we sinned, and upon which Christ died for our
salvation. If the Bible is to be a truly practical book, it is
difficult to understand how its emphasis could be otherwise.
At the same time the word הָאָרֶץ does not have precisely
the same connotation which it bore in verse one.[27] In the
first verse it went with the word הַשָּׁמַיִם to form a combination
which designates the well-ordered world and universe that we
now know. In verse two, however, it depicts the earth as
being in an uninhabitable condition. We might paraphrase
the thought, "The earth which we now know was at one time
in such a condition that men could not live upon it". The
word הָאָרֶץ is separated from what follows by means of the
disjunctive accent Rᵉbhîaʻ, and so we are to let our thought
dwell upon it before passing on to the following.[28]

The remainder of the first circumstantial clause forms a
predicate to הָאָרֶץ. We may render, "The earth — it was

---

inhabitants of the earth, and for religious ends; not to gratify curiosity,
but to strengthen faith in God, the Creator of the universe" (*op. cit.*,
p. 48). Aalders says, "zij (*i. e.*, the earth) is het, waarop wij mensen
wonen, waarop wij leven, lijden en sterven" (*op. cit.*, p. 78). I can see no
exegetical warrant for the remark in *La Sainte Bible*, Tome I, Iʳᵉ Partie,
Paris–VI, 1953, p. 104, "L'objet de la création divine est *le ciel et la terre*,
non pas la masse chaotique qui s'appelle tantôt *'areṣ*, terre".

[26] "Die kosmozentrische Betrachtung schlägt hier also plötzlich um in
die geozentrische, bei der es nun bleibt" (Procksch, *op. cit.*, p. 425).

[27] This is either explicitly acknowledged by many commentators or is a
justifiable conclusion to be deduced from their treatment of the word in
both verses. Ryle (*The Book of Genesis*, (*Cambridge Bible For Schools
and Colleges*), Cambridge, 1921, p. 3) interprets "the earth" as comprising
the materials out of which the universe is formed.

[28] It is the emphatic position of הָאָרֶץ which permits the interpretation
of Ridderbos (see note 24).

desolation and waste". This predicate describes the earth, not as it now is, but as it was once long ago. The copula is inserted for the purpose of stressing a condition which existed in past time, indeed at the time when God said, "Let there be light" (v. 3).[29] This condition is described by the two words תֹהוּ וָבֹהוּ i. e., "desolation and waste". The latter word never appears alone, but always in combination with תֹהוּ, usually following it immediately, being connected with it by the ordinary conjunction.[30] In one passage, however, namely, Isaiah 34:11, it is separated by another word. To determine the significance of תֹהוּ in Genesis 1:2 is not particularly difficult. In Isaiah 45:18 it is used as a contrast to the phrase, "to be inhabited". According to this verse God did not create the earth for desolation, but rather to be inhabited. An earth of תֹהוּ therefore, is an earth that cannot be inhabited. Such an earth has not fulfilled the purpose for which it was created; it is an earth created in vain, a desolate earth. If, therefore, we

[29] The copula is expressed only in the first of the three circumstantial clauses in order that all doubt may be removed that the reference is to past time. Childs (*op. cit.*, p. 32) comments that we have "a nominal clause of circumstantial force used to specify a condition in its proper sphere of time" and renders "the earth having been chaos". I do not believe that this rendering accurately reflects the force of the Hebrew or that it does justice to Childs' own evaluation of Genesis 1:2a. It leaves open room for the thought that "the earth having been chaos", was no longer chaos when God spoke. Grammatically we are to understand that at the very time when God said, "Let there be light", the earth was in the condition described in verse two. To be rejected also as reading too much into the Hebrew is the translation of Strack (*Die Genesis*, München, 1905, p. 1), "Die Erde aber war als Wüste und Leere geworden". Delitzsch (*op. cit.*, p. 77) remarks correctly, "The perfect thus preceded by its subject is the usual way of stating the circumstances under which a following narrative takes place". He then gives references to support this statement, and after discussing the accents of הָיְתָה asserts, "This הָיְתָה is no mere *erat*, it declares that the earth was found in a condition of תהו ובהו, when God's six-days' creative agency began".

[30] In a near open syllable the conjunction is often pointed with vocal Šᵉwā. Here, however, probably for the sake of assonance, it is pointed with Qāmetz. Nevertheless, this latter pointing is in accord with the fundamental rule that in a near open syllable the short *a* vowel must appear as Qāmetz.

34

translate as "desolation", we shall probably be doing justice to the word.[31]

Likewise, the similar sounding בֹהוּ apparently signifies something uninhabitable, and we may well render it as "waste".[32] Jeremiah uses this striking combination when describing the land of Palestine after it has been devastated by the invasion of Nebuchadnezzar's armies. At that time the land will become what it was at the beginning, a desolation and waste, so that man will no longer dwell therein. This is stressed in that the prophet depicts the birds as having flown away, the mountains being removed and the cities uprooted. On such an earth man cannot live. It is that thought which is also expressed in Genesis. The earth was in such a condition that man would have been unable to live thereon; it was desolation and waste.

A second circumstantial clause states that darkness was upon the face of the great deep. The reference of course is not to the oceans that we know but to the primeval waters which covered the earth. Over the face of these waters there was darkness. As the first word in this clause חֹשֶׁךְ is emphasized, it stands as a parallel to הָאָרֶץ in the previous clause. There are thus three principal subjects of the verse: the earth, darkness and the Spirit of God. The second clause in reality gives further support to the first. Man could not have lived upon the earth, for it was dark and covered by water.[33]

---

[31] LXX ἀόρατος, Aquila κένωμα, Theodotion κενόν, Symmachus ἀργόν, Onkelos צָדְיָא. Rosenmüller (*Scholia In Vetus Testamentum*, Pars Prima, Volumen Primum, Lipsiae, MDCCCXXI, p. 65) comments, "Quorum interpretum omnium mentibus obversatum esse patet τὸ χάος". He himself renders *vastitas*, and then correctly remarks, "Verba hebraea videntur nihil aliud designare, quam *inane*, quale est in regione deserta". In Ugaritic the root has been attested as *thw*.

[32] The word also occurs in Isa. 34:11; Jer. 4:23. It appears to be related to بَهِيَ *to be empty*.

[33] I can see no warrant for Childs' statement, "The darkness does not belong to God's creation, but is independent of it. It cannot be understood merely as the absence of light, but possesses a quality of its own" (*op. cit.*, p. 33). It is perfectly true, as Childs points out, that the concept darkness does bear theological significance. It is something else, however, to claim that here in Genesis 1:2 it is a positive something, not belonging to God's creation. In the nature of the case darkness is often suited to

From this verse alone we are not justified in saying that the earth was covered by water,[34] but later, in verse nine, the command is given that the dry land should appear. It would seem, then, that up until the time of the issuance of this command, the earth had actually been covered or surrounded by water.

---

symbolize affliction and death. Here, however, the darkness is merely one characteristic of the unformed earth. Man cannot live in darkness, and the first requisite step in making the earth habitable is the removal of darkness. This elementary fact must be recognized before we make any attempt to discover the theological significance of darkness. And it is well also to note that darkness is recognized in this chapter as a positive good for man. Whatever be the precise connotation of the עֶרֶב of each day, it certainly included darkness, and that darkness was for man's good. At times, therefore, darkness may typify evil and death; at other times it is to be looked upon as a positive blessing.

Ridderbos has an instructive footnote, "Indirekt wird es [*i. e.*, that God created the darkness] wohl gesagt (wenigstens bei meiner Auffassung von Vers 1), weil an Vers 2 der Ausspruch von Vers 1 vorangeht. Oder muss man sagen, dass die Finsternis von Vers 2 etwas rein Negatives ist? M.E. ist das nicht plausibel" (*op. cit.*, p. 239). Ridderbos calls attention to the fact that God gives the darkness a name and to the importance of name-giving in the Old Testament.

34 For an excellent discussion of the relationship between תְּהוֹם and Tiamat, *cf.* Alexander Heidel: *The Babylonian Genesis*,² Chicago, 1951, pp. 98–101. The exact philological equivalent of Tiamat in Hebrew would be תְּהוֹמָה. In the near open syllable unless a distant open syllable with a naturally long vowel precedes, *i* and *u* generally drop to Šᵉwā. The long *â* of Babylonian becomes Ḥōlem in Hebrew. If the two words are identical, the feminine ending has disappeared in the Hebrew. It should be noted that the Babylonian word tamtu, *sea*, may be written tiamtu. This again could be equated with תְּהוֹם. The difficulty lies in the disappearance of the feminine ending. The Babylonian equivalent of תְּהוֹם would be Tiâmu.

Childs is correct in interpreting תְּהוֹם of the primeval waters, but he has no warrant for asserting that they were uncreated (*op. cit.*, p. 33). It is true that no express mention is made of the creation of the waters, but the purpose of the entire first chapter of Genesis is to exalt God as the creator and to attribute the origin of all things to him. *Cf.* Oswald T. Allis: "Old Testament Emphases and Modern Thought" in *The Princeton Theological Review*, Vol. XXIII, No. 3 (July 1925), pp. 442 ff. The comment of Ridderbos is worth noting, "nur solange die Wasser innerhalb der Grenzen bleiben, die Gott ihnen angewiesen hat, sind sie unschädlich; wenn Gott zusteht, dass die Grenzen überschritten werden, sind es Mächte, die Tod und Verderben bringen, siehe Gen. vii 11; viii 2 (in beiden Fällen *tᵉhôm*) usw." (*op. cit.*, pp. 235 f.).

Lastly, the statement is made that the Spirit of God was hovering over the waters.[35] Although we shall have more to say on the subject later in an excursus, we may at this point note that the traditional translation, "Spirit of God", is accurate, whereas the proposed substitution, "a mighty wind", is not. Had Moses desired to speak of a mighty wind, why did he not employ the common expression רוּחַ גְּדוֹלָה which is found, for example, in Jonah 1:4 and Job 1:19? Secondly, the participle does not describe the blowing of a wind.[36]

---

[35] Maurer (Commentarius Grammaticus Criticus in Vetus Testamentum, Volumen Primum, Lipsiae, 1835, p. 1) says, "i. e. vis divina, qua moveri cuncta et animari opinata est prisca aetas". The word רוּחַ, as is well known, means breath, wind, spirit. Here it is the Spirit which is of God and which acts upon his creation. He is "the agent of the divine purpose in imparting life, and reducing the void, waste earth to order and clothing it with beauty" (J. Ritchie Smith: The Holy Spirit In The Gospels, New York, 1926, p. 34). Cf. my Excursus at conclusion of this article.

[36] The participle is best rendered in English as "hovering". In Jer. 23:9 the Qal means "to grow soft". The Arabic خَفَّ, also means "to grow soft". Whether this is the basic meaning of the Hebrew root, however, is difficult to determine. In the Pi'ēl, the root means "to hover". This is supported by Ugaritic, where the root also occurs in the II stem.

nšrm. trḫpn. ybṣr —
'eym. bn. nšrm. 'arḫp. an(k)

"the eagles will hover, the (flock of?) hawks will look upon him, among the eagles I shall hover" (Aqhat i:20, 21).

trpḫn. ybṣr. ḥbl. dey (m —)
nšrm. trḫp. 'nt.

"the eagles hovered over him, the flock of hawks looked down, and Anat hovered among the eagles" (Aqhat i:30, 32).

The eagles are here pictured as hovering over the prey, ready to dart down upon it.

Particularly instructive is Deut. 32:11 in which the Pi'ēl is also found. Israel is pictured as led by the Lord alone, and the Lord's action is compared to that of the eagle (נְשֶׁר cf. Ugaritic nšr) which "stirs up" its nest, forcing the young out so that they must fly, and then hovers (יְרַחֵף) over her young. The rendering "brood" is manifestly out of the question. Whatever be the precise conotation of the verb, it describes the actions of the mother eagle after the young are out of the nest or at least at the time when they are compelled to leave the nest. It is clear, therefore, that Genesis 1:2 is not speaking of a "mighty wind". The participle is unsuitable to describe the blowing of a wind.

Thirdly, mention of a mighty wind at this point would be out of place. Both the first and second clauses of the verse point out why man could not dwell upon the earth; they show that the earth at that time was not habitable. If the third clause simply states that a mighty wind was blowing over the waters, it does not contribute to showing that the earth was uninhabitable. It merely mentions an interesting detail, the purpose of which is difficult to ascertain.[37]

On the other hand, the traditional translation reveals that despite the fact that the earth was not then habitable, all was under the control of God's Spirit.[38] The Spirit is depicted as a living Being, who hovers over the created earth like a bird, and this statement is necessary for a proper understanding of the condition of things at that time.[39]

Were the conditions described in Genesis 1:2, however, such as God desired them to be? All too often the word

---

[37] It should be noted that whenever the phrase רוּחַ אֱלֹהִים occurs in the Old Testament, it refers to the Spirit of God and never to a mighty wind. *Cf.* Gen. 41:38; Ex. 31:3; 35:31; Num. 24:2; I Sam. 10:10; 16:14, 16; 18:10; 19:20, 23; I Chr. 24:20; Ez. 11:24. Note also רוּחַ יהוה in Jud. 3:10; 11:29; 13:25, *etc.*

[38] Thus Maurer (*op. cit.*, p. 1), "ita ut moles illa rudis atque indigesta sensim motum acciperet"; Keil (*op. cit.*, p. 49), "which worked upon the formless, lifeless mass, separating, quickening, and preparing the living forms, which were called into being by the creative words that followed". Frey appeals to John 4:24a and interprets רוּח as the longing of God ("seine Sehnsucht, das Gestaltlose, Gebundene, Finstere zu gestalten, zu befreien, und zum Ausdruck seines lichtvollen Gedanken zu machen" (*op. cit.*, p. 15). Calvin has gone to the heart of the matter (*Commentaries On The First Book of Moses Called Genesis*, Volume First, Grand Rapids, 1948, pp. 73 f.), "We have already heard that before God had perfected the world it was an indigested [indigestam] mass; he now teaches that the power of the Spirit was necessary in order to sustain it. For this doubt might occur to the mind, how such a disorderly heap could stand; seeing that we now behold the world preserved by government, or order. He therefore asserts that this mass, however confused it might be, was rendered stable, for the time, by the secret efficacy of the Spirit". Calvin aptly appeals to Psalm 104:29, 30.

[39] Procksch, however (*op. cit.*, p. 426), preferred to render רחף by brüten, and appealed to the Syriac ܟ̣ܒ, which has this meaning. רוּח he believes, is to be conceived as the power which awakens life. He would render the word "Gottesgeist" to emphasize the powerful, rather than the personal, in God.

"chaos" is applied to this condition, and when we today use that word, we are likely to do so under the more or less unconscious influence of Milton's *Paradise Lost*. It may be well to recall his lines,

> In the beginning how the heav'ns and earth
> Rose out of chaos . . . .

If then we employ this word "chaos" we must use it only as indicating the first stage in the formation of the present well-ordered earth and not as referring to what was confused and out of order, as though to suggest that the condition described in Genesis 1:2 was somehow out of God's control. All was well-ordered and precisely as God desired it to be.[40] There is no reason, so far as one can tell from reading the first chapter of Genesis, why God might not have pronounced the judgment, "very good", over the condition described in the second verse. The earth at that time was uninhabitable, but that same condition appears again during some of the later days of creation. Genesis 1:2 presents the first stage in the preparation of the earth for man. It stands out in remarkable contrast with the finished universe, as that is found in the thirty-first verse of the same chapter. It is the first picture of the created world that the Bible gives and the purpose of the remainder of the chapter is to show how God brought this world from its primitive condition of desolation and waste to become an earth, fully equipped to receive man and to be his home. The earth was desolation and waste, but all was in God's hand and under his control; nothing was contrary to his design.

EXCURSUS

"The Spirit of God" in Genesis 1:2

We have noted that von Rad rendered the phrase רוּחַ
אֱלֹהִים as "Gottessturm", *i. e.*, a fearful storm. His appeal to Daniel 7:2, however, we regarded as unjustified (see note 9, *supra*). Others have also rejected the common rendering

---

[40] *Cf.* Young: *op. cit.*, pp. 143 f.

"Spirit of God" and have interpreted the Hebrew as referring to an inanimate force such as the wind. It may be that this rendering goes back to the Targum Onkelos which translates וְרוּחָא מִן־קֳדָם־יְיָ מְנַשְּׁבָא עַל־אַפֵּי מַיָא: i. e., "and a wind from before the Lord was blowing upon the faces of the waters". In this Targum it is the participle which clearly shows that רוּחָא is to be translated "wind" and not "spirit".[41]

Apparently this rendering found favor also among many of the Jewish rabbis, if we may judge from the statement of Umberto Cassuto in his commentary on Genesis, "According to the interpretation of our Rabbis (Hagigah 12a) this רוּחַ is the wind, moving wind, air in motion, something created which God created on the first day".[42] Cassuto, himself, however, rejects this view as not being the plain meaning of the text.[43]

In recent times Professor Harry Orlinsky has written a cogent defense of the rendering "wind".[44] He asserts that a "systematic presentation and analysis of all the pertinent data will demonstrate the concept 'wind' and preclude 's/Spirit' ".[45] We shall seek to state and to evaluate his arguments.

1. Orlinsky believes that the "biblical version of Creation . . . derives ultimately and in significant measure" from the Mesopotamian versions, and in these latter the wind plays a significant role.[46] In Enuma Elish, for example, Anu begets the four winds, which are associated with Tiamat, and were created before the universe. Orlinsky appeals also to other ancient cosmogonies, but, inasmuch as he regards Genesis as sustaining a relation to Enuma Elish, we shall pay particular attention to that document.

[41] Both the Jerusalem Targum and that of Pseudo-Jonathan have added דְרַחֲמִין to the word רוּחָא.

[42] Umberto Cassuto: A Commentary On The Book of Genesis (in Hebrew), 1953, Part I, p. 13, לפי דרש רבותינו (חגינה י"ב ע"א) רוח זו הריהי רוח ממש, אויר. מתנועע, בריאה שבראה אלהים ביום הראשון:

[43] Op. cit., p. 13, אבל אין זה נראה פשוטו של מקרא.

[44] Harry M. Orlinsky: "The Plain Meaning of RUAH in Gen. 1.2" in The Jewish Quarterly Review, Volume XLVIII, 1957–1958, Philadelphia, pp. 174–182. Orlinsky's article is particularly valuable for its references to the relevant literature.

[45] Op. cit., p. 177.

[46] Op. cit., pp. 177–178.

In the first place we must emphasize the fact that Genesis one and Enuma Elish are two entirely different types of document and do not belong to the same literary genre. Genesis one is a semi-poetic account of creation, told as straightforward narration.[47] The great central theme of the chapter is the fact of God's creating heaven and earth and his monergism in preparing the earth for man's habitancy. Enuma Elish on the other hand is a nature myth in which elements of "creation" are more or less incidental. It lacks a statement of absolute creation such as is found in Genesis 1:1 and it lacks an account of progress in the preparation of the earth such as occurs in the remainder of Genesis one.

Secondly, even if רוּחַ אֱלֹהִים contrary to biblical usage elsewhere, were to be rendered "a mighty wind", there would still be nothing comparable to this conception in Enuma Elish. The "wind of God moving over the face of the water", as Professor Orlinsky translates, is a thought wholly foreign to Enuma Elish. After Marduk was born, Anu created the four winds to restrain the host of monsters (Tablet I, lines 105, 106). Nothing more is said about these winds in Tablet I. In Tablet IV, however, occurs the statement, "Go, and cut off the life of Ti'âmat. May the winds carry her blood to out-of-the-way places" (lines 31, 32).[48] As Marduk sets out to destroy Tiamat, the four winds aid him. These are now named, "the south, the north, the east and the west wind" (lines 42, 43). We are then told of the creation of the imḫullu, the evil wind, cyclone, hurricane, etc. (lines 45, 46). Then follows the statement, "He sent forth the winds which he had created, the seven of them; to trouble Ti'âmat within, they arose behind him".[49]

In the actual conflict Marduk let loose the evil wind in Tiamat's face and drove this wind into Tiamat's mouth, and thus the raging winds filled her belly (lines 96–99). The north wind served later to carry off some remains of Tiamat to

---

[47] We use the term semi-poetic merely to stress the elevated character of the language. Inasmuch as true parallelism in the verses is lacking Genesis one cannot legitimately be designated poetry in the Hebrew sense.

[48] Translation of Alexander Heidel (*op. cit.*, p. 37).

[49] Translation of Heidel (*op. cit.*, p. 38).

distant places (line 132).⁵⁰ How different from Genesis! Instead of one wind we have seven, and that wind which aids in the destruction of the monster is called an evil wind. In Genesis, however, the genitive אֱלֹהִים is used. If Genesis is speaking of a wind, it is a wind of God, not an evil wind used to aid in the destruction of a creature. Even if the words be rendered "mighty wind" there is no indication that this wind was harmful. Furthermore, the action of רוּחַ has to do only with the waters and not with the תְהוֹם as we might expect, if there had been actual dependence upon Enuma Elish. The mention of winds in Enuma Elish, therefore, is no support for the rendering "wind of God" in Genesis 1:2.

2. The LXX is said to have taken רוּחַ in the sense of "wind" or "breath", καὶ πνεῦμα θεοῦ ἐπεφέρετο ἐπάνω τοῦ ὕδατος. To support this position appeal is made to Genesis 8:1. It may readily be granted that πνεῦμα can mean "wind". The question is whether that is the way the Septuagint should here be understood. It depends upon the force of the verb ἐπεφέρετο. This verb is passive and should be translated, "was brought". The πνεῦμα then is something that was being brought above the water. It is difficult to tell what the translator of Codex B had in mind. It should be noted, however, that the Vulgate renders, "et spiritus Dei ferebatur super aquas". The word "ferebatur" (ἐπεφέρετο), therefore, may easily be used with "Spirit" as subject. We conclude that the LXX rendering of Genesis 1:2 does not demand that πνεῦμα be rendered "wind".

3. Appeal is also made to the Targum whose rendering has already been noted (see first paragraph of present Excursus).

4. Professor Orlinsky appeals to Rab Judah, an Amora of Babylonia, from the third century A.D., who states that on the first day ten things were created, among which he lists רוח ומים which Orlinsky renders "wind and water". If this interpretation is correct, it merely shows that the rendering "wind" among Jewish scholars was very old.

5. The interpretation of רוּחַ as "wind" is said to fit in well with the role of רוּחַ in the creation story generally. In

---

⁵⁰ It is difficult to determine precisely what it was that the north wind was to carry off.

Genesis 3:8 the word refers to the breeze of the day, and in 6:17 and 7:15 it is to be given as "breath of life". These passages, however, do not determine the significance of רוּחַ in 1:2, for they are too far removed from its immediate context.

What rules out the rendering "wind" in Genesis 1:2 is the participle. Orlinsky thinks that the רוּחַ is no more active than any of the other elements mentioned (*op. cit.*, p. 180). But מְרַחֶפֶת is an active participle whose subject is actively engaged. We have already discussed the meaning of this participle and seen that it is not an appropriate word to employ in describing wind. The unformed earth will not be destroyed for the Spirit who belongs to the God (אֱלֹהִים) who created heaven and earth is hovering over it. There is no need to introduce the Spirit later in the chapter. Over the unformed earth the Spirit moves until God is ready to call the light into existence. Having mentioned this fact, Moses goes on to direct our thought to the work of God in transforming the unformed earth into our present world.

THE DAYS OF GENESIS

"WE do not read in the Gospel", declared Augustine, "that the Lord said, 'I send to you the Paraclete who will teach you about the course of the sun and the moon'; for he wanted to make Christians, not mathematicians".[1] Commenting on these words, Bavinck remarked that when the Scripture, as a book of religion, comes into contact with other sciences and sheds its light upon them, it does not then suddenly cease to be God's Word but continues to be such. Furthermore, he added, "when it speaks about the origin of heaven and earth, it presents no saga or myth or poetical fantasy but even then, according to its clear intention, presents history, which deserves faith and trust. And for that reason, Christian theology, with but few exceptions, has held fast to the literal, historical view of the account of creation."[2]

It is of course true that the Bible is not a textbook of science, but all too often, it would seem, this fact is made a pretext for treating lightly the content of Genesis one. Inasmuch as the Bible is the Word of God, whenever it speaks on any subject, whatever that subject may be, it is accurate in what it says. The Bible may not have been given to teach science as such, but it does teach about the origin of all things, a ques-

[1] "Non legitur in Evangelio Dominum dixisse: Mitto vobis Paracletum qui vos doceat de cursu solis et lunae. Christianos enim facere volebat, non mathematicos" ("De Actis Cum Felice Manichaeo", *Patrologia Latina*, XLII, col. 525, caput X).

[2] "Maar als de Schrift dan toch van haar standpunt uit, juist als boek der religie, met andere wetenschappen in aanraking komt en ook daarover haar licht laat schijnen, dan houdt ze niet eensklaps op Gods Woord te zijn maar blijft dat. Ook als ze over de wording van hemel en aarde spreekt, geeft ze geen sage of mythe of dichterlijke phantasie, maar ook dan geeft zij naar hare duidelijke bedoeling historie, die geloof en vertrouwen verdient. En daarom hield de Christelijke theologie dan ook, op schlechts enkele uitzonderingen na, aan de letterlijke, historische opvatting van het scheppingsverhall vast" (Herman Bavinck: *Gereformeerde Dogmatiek*, Tweede Deel, Kampen, 1928, p. 458).

44

tion upon which many scientists apparently have little to say. At the present day Bavinck's remarks are particularly in order, for recently there has appeared a recrudescence of the so-called "framework" hypothesis of the days of Genesis, an hypothesis which in the opinion of the writer of this article treats the content of Genesis one too lightly and which, at least according to some of its advocates, seems to rescue the Bible from the position of being in conflict with the data of modern science.[3] The theory has found advocacy recently both by Roman Catholics and by evangelical Protestants.[4] It is the purpose of the present article to discuss this hypothesis as it has been presented by some of its most able exponents.

I. Professor Noordtzij and the "Framework" Hypothesis

In 1924 Professor Arie Noordtzij of the University of Utrecht published a work whose title may be translated, God's Word and the Testimony of the Ages.[5] It is in many

[3] Strack, for example (*Die Genesis*, 1905, p. 9), wrote, "sie (*i. e.*, what Strack calls "die ideale Auffassung") hat den grossen Vorteil, dass sie bei dem Ver. nicht naturwissenschaftliche Kenntnisse voraussetzt, die er aller Wahrscheinlichkeit nach so wenig wie irgendeiner seiner Zeitgenossen gehabt hat, und indem sie der Bibel wie der Naturwissenschaft volles Recht lässt in Bezug auf das jeder eigentümliche Gebiet, hat sie doch keinen Konflikt zwischen beiden zur Folge". Professor N. H. Ridderbos, who has written one of the fullest recent discussions of the "framework" hypothesis entitles the English translation of his work, Is There a Conflict Between Genesis 1 and Natural Science?, Grand Rapids, 1957. The original work bears the title, *Beschouwingen over Genesis I*, Assen.

[4] See J. O. Morgan: *Moses and Myth*, London, 1932; N. H. Ridderbos: *op. cit.*; Meredith G. Kline: "Because It Had Not Rained", *Westminster Theological Journal*, Vol. XX, No. 2 (May 1958), pp. 146–157; Bernard Ramm: *The Christian View of Science and Scripture*, Grand Rapids, 1954, which gives a useful summary of various views (see pp. 222–229).

[5] A. Noordtzij: *Gods Woord en der Eeuwen Getuigenis. Het Oude Testament in het Licht der Oostersche Opgravingen*, Kampen, 1924. In "Vragen Rondom Genesis en de Naturwetenschappen", *Bezinning*, 17e Jaargang, 1962, No. 1, pp. 21 ff., attention is called to the position of Noordtzij. The position is described as figurative (figuurlijke), and is opposed by adducing the following considerations. 1.) The clear distinction between Genesis 1 on the one hand and Genesis 2 and 3 in itself is not sufficient ground for assuming that one section is to be taken literally, the other not. 2.) Did the writer of this part of Genesis really desire to make a hard and

respects a remarkable book and contains a useful discussion of the relationship between the Old Testament and archaeological discoveries. Noordtzij has some interesting things to say about the days of Genesis. The Holy Scripture, so he tells us, always places the creation in the light of the central fact of redemption, Christ Jesus.[6] When we examine the first chapter of Genesis in the light of other parts of Scripture, it becomes clear that the intention is not to give a survey of the process of creation, but to permit us to see the creative activity of God in the light of his saving acts, and so, in its structure, the chapter allows its full light to fall upon man, the crown of the creative work.[7]

Inasmuch as the heaven is of a higher order than the earth it is not subject to a development as is the earth.[8] It rather possesses its own character and is not to be placed on the same plane as the earth. The order of visible things is bound up with space and time, but not that of invisible things. Nor does the Scripture teach a creation *ex nihilo*, but one out of God's will.[9]

That the six days do not have to do with the course of a natural process may be seen, thinks Noordtzij, from the

fast distinction between the creation account and what follows? The objection is summarized: "Sammenvattend zou men kunnen zeggen, dat het argument: de schepping is iets totaal anders dan het begin der menschengeschiedenis en daarom kan men Genesis 1 anders opvatten dan Genesis 2 en 3, minder sterk is dan het lijkt" (pp. 23 f.).

[6] "Der H. S. stelt het feit der schepping steeds in het licht van het centrale heilsfeit der verlossing, die in Christus Jezus is, hetzij Hij in het Oude Verbond profetisch wordt aangekondigd, hetzij die verlossing als uitgangspunt voor de eschatalogische ontwikkeling wordt gegrepen" (*op. cit.*, p. 77).

[7] "Zoo dikwijls men echter Gen. 1 beschouwt in het licht van de andere gedeelten der H. S., wordt het duidelijk, dat hier niet de bedoeling voorzit om ons een overzicht te geven van het scheppingsproces, maar om ons de scheppende werkzaamheid Gods te doen zien in het licht zijner heilsgedachten, waarom het dan ook door zijn structuur het volle licht doet vallen op den mensch, die als de kroon is van het scheppingswerk" (*op. cit.*, pp. 77 f.).

[8] "Maar nu is de hemel, wijl van een andere en hoogere orde dan deze aarde, niet aan ontwikkeling onderworpen gelijk deze aarde" (*op. cit.*, p. 78).

[9] "De H. S. leert ons dan ook niet een „scheppen uit niets" maar een scheppen uit een kracht: de wil Gods (*Openb.* 4:11)" (*op. cit.*, p. 79).

manner in which the writer groups his material. We are given two trios which exhibit a pronounced parallelism, all of which has the purpose of bringing to the fore the preeminent glory of man, who actually reaches his destiny in the sabbath, for the sabbath is the point in which the creative work of God culminates and to which it attains.[10] The six days show that the process of origins is to be seen in the light of the highest and last creation of this visible world, namely, man, and with man the entire cosmos is placed in the light of the seventh day and so in the light of dedication to God himself.[11] What is significant is not the concept "day", taken by itself, but rather the concept of "six plus one".

Inasmuch as the writer speaks of evenings and mornings previous to the heavenly bodies of the fourth day, continues Noordtzij, it is clear that he uses the terms "days" and "nights" as a framework (kader). Such a division of time is a projection not given to show us the account of creation in its natural historical course, but, as elsewhere in the Holy Scriptures, to exhibit the majesty of the creation in the light of the great saving purpose of God.[12] The writer takes his

[10] "De schepping is aangelegd op het groote, geestelijke goed, dat zich in de sabbatsgedachte belichaamt. Daarom en daarom alleen is er in Gen. 1 van 6 dagen sprake, waarop de sabbat volgt als de dag bij uitnemendheid, wijl het Gods dag is" (*op. cit.*, p. 81).

[11] "dat Genesis 1 het wordingsproces ziet in het licht van het hoogste en laatste schepsel dezer zichtbare wereld: den mensch, en dat met dien mensch heel de kosmos gesteld wordt in het licht van den 7den dag en dus in het licht van de wijding aan God zelven" (*op. cit.*, p. 79). Even if the entire emphasis, however, were to fall upon the seventh day, it would not follow that the six days did not correspond to reality. On the contrary, the reality of the sabbath as a creation ordinance is grounded upon the reality of the six days' work. If the seventh day does not correspond to reality, the basis for observance of the sabbath is removed. Note the connection in Exodus 20:8 ff., "Remember the day of the Sabbath to keep it holy," "and he rested on the seventh day."

It should further be noted that the phrase הַשַּׁבָּת יוֹם is not used in Genesis 1:1–2:3, nor is there anything in the text which shows that the six days are mentioned merely for the sake of emphasizing the concept of the sabbath. Man, it is well to remember, was not made for the sabbath, but the sabbath for man (*cf.* Mk. 2:27). Genesis 1:1–2:3 says nothing about man's relation to the sabbath. Man was not created for the sabbath, but to rule the earth.

[12] "De tijdsindeeling is een projectie, gebezigd *niet* om ons het scheppingsverhaal in zijn natuurhistorisch verloop te teekenen maar om evenals elders

expressions from the full and rich daily life of his people, for the Holy Spirit always speaks the words of God in human language. Why then, we may ask, are the six days mentioned? The answer, according to Noordtzij, is that they are only mentioned to prepare us for the seventh day. In reply to this interpretation, the late Professor G. C. Aalders of the Free University of Amsterdam had some cogent remarks to make. Desirous as he was of being completely fair to Noordtzij, Aalders nevertheless declared that he was compelled to understand Noordtzij as holding that as far as the days of Genesis are concerned, there was no reality with respect to the divine creative activity.[13] Aalders then adduced two considerations which must guide every serious interpreter of the first chapter of Genesis. (1) In the text of Genesis itself, he affirmed, there is not a single allusion to suggest that the days are to be regarded as a form or mere manner of representation and hence of no significance for the essential knowledge of the divine creative activity. (2) In Exodus 20:11 the activity of God is presented to man as a pattern, and this fact presupposes that there was a reality in the activity of God which man is to follow. How could man be held accountable for working six days if God himself had not actually worked for six days?[14] To the best of the present writer's knowledge no one has ever answered these two considerations of Aalders.

in de H.S. ons de heerlijkheid der schepselen te teekenen in het licht van het groote heilsdoel Gods" (*op. cit.*, p. 80).

[13] "Wij kunnen dit niet anders verstaan dat ook naar het oordeel van Noordtzij aan de „dagen" geen realiteit in betrekking tot de Goddelijke scheppingswerkzaamheid toekomt" (G. Ch. Aalders: *De Goddelijke Openbaring in de eerste drie Hoofdstukken van Genesis*, Kampen, 1932, p. 233).

[14] "1°, dat de tekst van Gen. 1 zelf geen enkele aanvijzing bevat, dat de dagen slechts als een vorm of voorstellingswijze zouden bedoeld zijn en derhalve voor de wezenlijke kennis van de Goddelijke scheppingswerkzaamheid geen waarde zouden hebben: en 2° dat in Ex. 20:11 het doen Gods aan den mensch tot voorbeeld wordt gesteld; en dit veronderstelt zeer zeker, dat in dat doen Gods een realiteit is geweest, welke door den mensch hun worden nagevolgd. Hoe zou den mensch kunnen worden voorgehouden dat hij na zes dagen arbeiden op den zevenden dag moet rusten, omdat God in zes dagen alle dingen geschapen heeft en rustte op den zevenden dag, indien aan die zes scheppingsdagen in het Goddelijk scheppingswerk geen enkele realiteit beantwoordde?" (*op. cit.*, p. 232).

48

II. *Preliminary Remarks About Genesis One*

Before we attempt to evaluate the arguments employed in defense of a non-chronological view of the days of Genesis one, it is necessary to delineate briefly what we believe to be the nature of the Bible's first chapter. We may begin by asking whether Genesis one is a special revelation from God in the sense that it is a communication of information to man from God concerning the subjects of which it treats. This question has been answered in the negative by John L. McKenzie, S.J. in a recent article. "It is not a tenable view that God in revealing Himself also revealed directly and in detail the truth about such things as creation and the fall of man; the very presence of so many mythical elements in their traditions is enough to eliminate such a view".[15] If, however, this view of special revelation cannot be held, what alternative does Professor McKenzie offer? The alternative, it would seem, is to look upon Genesis one as in reality a human composition, although McKenzie does not use just these terms. According to him Genesis one is a retreatment of a known myth, in which the writer has radically excised the mythical elements and has "written an explicit polemic against the creation myth". The polytheism, theogony, theomachy and the "creative combat" are removed so that now the act of creation is "achieved in entire tranquility".[16]

What then are we to call the first chapter of Genesis after these various pagan elements have been excised? It is not history for "it is impossible to suppose that he (*i. e.*, the Hebrew) had historical knowledge of either of these events" (*i. e.*, either of the creation or the deluge).[17] Nor can Genesis one really be called a theological reconstruction or interpretation.[18] What then is this first chapter of Genesis? Actually

[15] John L. McKenzie, S.J.: "Myth and the Old Testament", in *The Catholic Biblical Quarterly*, Vol. XXI, July 1959, p. 281.

[16] *Op. cit.*, p. 277. This position is widely held; *cf.* Young, "The Interpretation of Genesis 1:2", *Westminster Theological Journal*, Vol. XXIII, May 1961, pp. 151–178, where references to relevant literature will be found.

[17] *Op. cit.*, p. 278.

[18] But *cf.* Gerhard von Rad: *Das erste Buch Mose, Genesis Kapitel 1–25, 18*, 1953, p. 36, "es (*i. e.*, the creation account) ist Lehre, die in langsamsten,

it is a story which the Hebrews told in place of the story which it displaced. It is not, however, a single story, but rather represents a multiple approach, and each of its images has value as an intuition of creation's reality. These images are symbolic representations of a reality which otherwise would not be known or expressed. The knowledge of God the Hebrews possessed through the revelation of himself, and in their handling of the creation account they sought to remove everything that was out of accord with their conception of God. They did possess a knowledge of God but, even so, the unknown remained unknown and mysterious. In speaking of the unknown, therefore, all the Hebrews could do was "to represent through symbolic forms the action of the unknown reality which they perceived mystically, not mythically, through His revelation of Himself".[19]

McKenzie's rejection of the view that Genesis one is a special revelation from the one living and true God is somewhat facile. He brings only one argument against that position, namely, the assumption that there are mythological elements in the first chapter of the Bible.[20]

Elsewhere we have sought to demonstrate the untenableness of the view that there are mythical elements in the first chapter of the Bible.[21]

If, however, one rejects the position that Genesis one is a special revelation of God, as Professor McKenzie does, a number of pertinent questions remain unanswered. For one thing, why cannot God have revealed to man the so-called area of the unknown? Why, in other words, can God not have told man in simple language just what God did in creating the heaven and the earth?[22] What warrant is there for the

jahrhundertelangem Wachstum sich behutsam angereichert hat". Despite this sentence, it is not clear that the positions of von Rad and McKenzie are essentially different.

[19] *Op. cit.*, p. 281.

[20] K. Popma: "Enkele voorslagen betreffende de exegese van Genesis 1–3", in *Lucerna*, 3° Jaargang, no. 2, p. 632, speaks of this as exegesis "die haar naam niet meer waard is; t.w. diverse opvattingen van sage, mythe, e.d.".

[21] *Cf.* Young: *op. cit.*

[22] In *Bezinning, loc. cit.*, p. 23, the wholesome remark is made, "welke daad Gods, op welk moment in de menselijke historie, is niet te wonderlijk

50

assumption that the unknown could only be represented through symbolic forms? Furthermore, if the Hebrews were guided in their handling of the creation by the conceptions of God which they held, whence did they obtain those conceptions? Were they communicated in words from God himself, as when he said, "Ye shall therefore be holy, for I am holy" (Leviticus 11:45b), or did they adopt them as a result of their reaction to events in the world which they thought represented the acting of God in power? How could the Hebrews know that the conceptions of God which they possessed actually corresponded to reality?

McKenzie's article shows what difficulties arise when one rejects the historic position of the Christian Church, and indeed of the Bible itself, that Scripture, in the orthodox sense, is the Word of God and a revelation from him. As soon as one makes the assumption that Genesis one is really the work of man, he is hard pressed to discover the lessons that the chapter can teach. If the work is of human origination, how can it have a theological message or be regarded in any sense as the Word of God?

The position adopted in this article is that the events recorded in the first chapter of the Bible actually took place. They were historical events, and Genesis one, therefore, is to be regarded as historical. In employing the word "historical", we are rejecting the definition which would limit the word to that which man can know through scientific investigation alone.[23] We are using the word rather as including all

om haar enigermate letterlijk in onze taal te beschrijven? Is de vleeswording des Woords, is de bekering van ons hart minder wonderlijk dan de schepping van hemel en aarde?" Those who reject the historic Christian position that Scripture is a special revelation from God and yet still wish to regard the Scripture as the Word of God have no adequate criterion by which to judge the nature of Scripture. Thus, Ralph H. Elliott, *The Message of Genesis*, Nashville, 1961, p. 13, remarks that creation was event, and that it was up to succeeding generations to translate this event into meaning "as they analyzed the event and as they comprehended God". But how can one be sure that they analyzed the event correctly or that they comprehended God correctly unless God himself told them how to do this?

[23] Cf. e. g., W. F. Albright: *From the Stone Age to Christianity*. New York, 1957, p. 399, and a discussion of this view in Young: *Thy Word Is Truth*, Grand Rapids, 1957, pp. 245 ff.

which has transpired. Our knowledge of the events of creation we receive through the inscripturated revelation of God. The defense of this position will be made as the argument progresses. At this point, however, it may be well to note that the New Testament looks upon certain events of the creative week as genuinely historical. The creation itself is attributed to the Word of God (Hebrews 11:3), and Peter refers to the emerging of the earth as something that had actually taken place (II Peter 3:5b).[24] There is no question in Paul's mind about the historicity of God's first fiat (II Corinthians 4:6). According to Paul, the same God who commanded the light to shine out of darkness has also shined in the hearts of believers. Hebrews 6:7[25] seems to reflect upon the bringing forth of herbs on the third day, and Acts 17:24 to the work of filling the earth with its inhabitants. Likewise I Corinthians 11:7 asserts that man is the image of God, and his creation is specifically mentioned in Matthew 19:4.

It is furthermore necessary to say a word about the relationship between Scripture and science. For one thing it is difficult to escape the impression that some of those who espouse a non-chronological view of the days of Genesis are moved by a desire to escape the difficulties which exist between Genesis and the so-called "findings" of science.[26] That such difficulties

[24] Commenting on II Peter 3:5b, Bigg, (*The International Critical Commentary*, New York, 1922, p. 293) remarks, "Ἐξ may be taken to denote the emerging of the earth from the waters (Gen. i.9) in which it had lain buried, and the majority of commentators appear to adopt this explanation". Bigg, himself, however, thinks that the reference is to the material from which the earth was made. In this interpretation we think that Bigg is mistaken. What is clear, however, is that Peter is referring to the event in Genesis, as something that actually occurred. To Peter the event which he describes as γῆ ἐξ ὕδατος καὶ δι' ὕδατος συνεστῶσα was just as historical as that which he relates in the words δι' ὧν ὁ τότε κόσμος ὕδατι κατακλυσθεὶς ἀπώλετο.

[25] James Moffatt (*The International Critical Commentary*, New York, 1924, p. 81) thinks that Hebrews 6:7 contains reminiscences of the words of Genesis 1:12.

[26] Cf. Morgan: *op. cit.*, pp. 17–46. The chronological order of Genesis is thought to be practically the reverse of that of geology (p. 36). Morgan mentions four attempts to "effect a conciliation between the postulates of the natural sciences and the Mosaic cosmogony" (p. 36). One of these is described as ingenious, "but it must inevitably prove unacceptable to the scientist" (p. 37). The *Idealist* theory in its various forms is said to

52

do exist cannot be denied, and their presence is a concern to every devout and thoughtful student of the Bible.[27] It is for this reason that one must do full justice both to Scripture and to science.

Recently there has been making its appearance in some evangelical circles the view that God has, in effect, given one revelation in the Bible and another in nature. Each of these in its own sphere is thought to be authoritative. It is the work of the theologian to interpret Scripture and of the scientist to interpret nature. "Whenever", as Dr. John Whitcomb describes it, "there is apparent conflict between the conclusions of the scientist and the conclusions of the theologian, especially with regard to such problems as the origin of the universe, solar system, earth, animal life, and man; the effects of the Edenic curse; and the magnitude and effects of the Noahic Deluge, the theologian must rethink his interpretation of the Scriptures at these points in such a way as to bring it into harmony with the general consensus of scientific opinion on these matters, since the Bible is not a textbook on science, and these problems overlap the territory in which science alone must give us the detailed and authoritative answers".[28]

It would be difficult to state this approach more concisely and accurately. One manifestation thereof may be found in a recent issue of *Bezinning*, in which the entire number is de-

be more satisfactory, and Lattey's view (*i. e.*, a form of the non-chronological hypothesis) is described as "eminently satisfying" (p. 39).

[27] It certainly cannot be expected of any mere man that he possess sufficient knowledge to state accurately the full relationship between Genesis and the study of God's created phenomena, let alone that he be expected to resolve whatever difficulties may appear. A truly humble student will acknowledge his ignorance and will make it his aim to be faithful to the holy and infallible words of Scripture. Many of the alleged difficulties, such as the creation of light before the sun, are really not basic difficulties at all, for there are at hand reasonable explanations thereof. And let it be remembered that scientists often adduce as "facts" that which, as a result of further research, turns out not to be fact at all. The treatment of this question in *Bezinning* (*loc. cit.*, especially pp. 16 ff.) is in many respects unsatisfactory and disappointing.

[28] John C. Whitcomb, Jr.: *Biblical Inerrancy and the Double Revelation Theory*, Presidential Address given at the Seventh General Meeting of the Midwestern Section of the Evangelical Theological Society, May 4, 1962, Moody Bible Institute.

voted to the subject, "Questions Concerning Genesis and the Sciences".[29] In the introduction to this work we are told that a conflict between Genesis and science can only be avoided when we maintain that the Bible is not a textbook of science but "salvation-history", and that the writers of the Bible spoke with the language and in the pictures of their time.[30] What strikes one immediately upon reading such a statement is the low estimate of the Bible which it entails. Whenever "science" and the Bible are in conflict, it is always the Bible that, in one manner or another, must give way. We are not told that "science" should correct its answers in the light of Scripture. Always it is the other way round. Yet this is really surprising, for the answers which scientists have provided have frequently changed with the passing of time. The "authoritative" answers of pre-Copernican scientists are no longer acceptable; nor, for that matter, are many of the views of twenty-five years ago.

To enter into a full critique of this thoroughly unscriptural and, therefore, untenable position, would be out of place in the present article.[31] There is, however, one consideration that must be noted, namely, that the approach which we are now engaged in discussing is one which leaves out of account the noetic effects of sin. It is true that the heavens declare the glory of God, but the eyes of man's understanding, blinded by sin, do not read the heavens aright. The noetic effects of sin lead to anti-theistic presuppositions and inclinations. We must remember that much that is presented as scientific fact

---

[29] *Op. cit.*, pp. 1–57.

[30] "Een conflict tussen Genesis en wetenschap kan natuurlijk in ieder geval worden vermeden wanneer men vasthoudt dat de Bijbel geen handboek is voor natuurwetenschap, maar Heilshistorie, en dat volgens het woord van Calvijn, God in de H. Schrift tot ons spreekt als een moeder tot haar kinderen" (*op. cit.*, p. 2). *Cf.* Herman Ridderbos' discussion, "Belangrijke publikatie" in *Gereformeerd Weekblad*, Zeventiende Jaargang, Nr. 40, p. 314, and the valuable remarks of Visée, in *Lucerna, loc. cit.*, pp. 638–639. Particularly timely is his comment, "De Schrift verhaalt ons heilsfeiten, maar deze waarheid houdt ook in dat we hier met feiten te doen hebben" (p. 639).

[31] *Cf.* Cornelius Van Til: *The Defense of the Faith*, Phila., 1955. Visée (*op. cit.*, p. 641) rightly applies the old and pertinent rule, "Lees wat er staat, en versta wat ge leest".

is written from a standpoint that is hostile to supernatural Christianity.

In the nature of the case God's revelation does not conflict with itself. His revelation in nature and that in Scripture are in perfect accord. Man, however, is a rational creature, and needs a revelation in words that he may properly understand himself and his relation to the world in which he lives. Even in his unfallen state, God gave to Adam a word-revelation, for by his very constitution as an intellectual being, man must have such. The word-revelation, therefore, must interpret revelation in nature. Fallen man must read general revelation in the light of Scripture, else he will go basically astray. Of course the Bible is not a textbook of science, but the Bible is necessary properly to understand the purpose of science. Perhaps one may say that it is a textbook of the philosophy of science. And on whatever subject the Bible speaks, whether it be creation, the making of the sun, the fall, the flood, man's redemption, it is authoritative and true. We are to think God's thoughts after him, and his thoughts are expressed in the words of Scripture. When these thoughts have to do with the origin of man, we are to think them also. They alone must be our guide. "Therefore", says Calvin, "while it becomes man seriously to employ his eyes in considering the works of God, since a place has been assigned him in this most glorious theatre that he may be a spectator of them, his special duty is to give ear to the Word, that he may the better profit".[32] And what Calvin so beautifully states, God himself had already made known to us through the Psalmist, "The entrance of thy words giveth light" (Psalm 119:130).

By way of summary we may state the three basic considerations which will undergird the position adopted in this article.

1. Genesis one is a special revelation from God.
2. Genesis one is historical; it relates matters which actually occurred.
3. In the nature of the case, general revelation is to be interpreted by special revelation, nature by Scripture, "science" by the Bible.

[32] *Institutes of the Christian Religion*, Grand Rapids, 1953, I:vi:2, p. 66, translated by Henry Beveridge.

III. *Evaluation of Arguments used to Defend the "Framework" Hypothesis*

1. The Use of Anthropomorphic Language

In defense of the non-chronological hypothesis it is argued that God speaks anthropomorphically. "Is . . . the author not under the necessity", asks Professor N. H. Ridderbos, "of employing such a method, because this is the only way to speak about something that is really beyond all human thoughts and words?"[33] And again, "Does the author mean to say that God completed creation in six days, or does he make use of an anthropomorphic mode of presentation?"[34]

If we understand this argument correctly, it is that the mention of six days is merely an anthropomorphic way of speaking. We are not to interpret it, as did Luther and Calvin, to mean that God actually created in six days, but merely to regard it as an anthropomorphic mode of speech. Genesis 2:7, for example, speaks of God forming the body of man of dust from the ground, but this does not mean that God acted as a potter, nor does Genesis 3:21 in stating that God clothed Adam and his wife mean to say that God acted as a "maker of fur-clothes". Again, when we are told that God rested (Genesis 2:2) are we to infer that "God had to exert Himself to create the world?"[35]

It is of course true that the term "anthropomorphism" has often been employed with reference to such phrases as "the mouth of the Lord", "and God said", "and God saw", and other similar expressions.[36] It is certainly true that God did not

[33] "The Meaning of Genesis I", in *Free University Quarterly*, Vol. IV, 1955/1957, p. 222 (hereafter abbreviated *Quarterly*).

[34] *Is There A Conflict Between Genesis 1 And Natural Science?*, p. 30 (hereafter abbreviated *Conflict*). Ridderbos gives three examples of "anthropomorphisms".

[35] *Op. cit.*, p. 30.

[36] A series of penetrating articles on the question of anthropomorphism by G. Visée appeared in *De Reformatie* (28e Jaargang, Nos. 34–43, 1953) under the title "Over het anthropomorphe spreken Gods in de heilige Schrift". He concludes that to talk of an "anthropomorphic" revelation in the usual sense of the word is not justifiable, and that it is better not to use the term. In *Lucerna* (*loc. cit.*, pp. 636 f.) he writes, "Ik ontken en bestrijd heel de idee van een ,,anthropomorphe" openbaring. God heeft

56

speak with physical organs of speech nor did he utter words in the Hebrew language. Are we, however, for that reason, to come to the conclusion that the language is merely figurative and does not designate a specific divine activity or reality? If we were so to conclude we would not be doing justice to the Scriptures. The phrases which have just been quoted are not devoid of significance and meaning. Rather, the statement, "and God said", to take one example, represents a genuine activity upon the part of God, a true and effectual speaking which accomplishes his will.[37] There are at least two reasons which substantiate this conclusion. In the first place genuine content is attributed to God's speaking, namely, the words, "Let there be light". This is strengthened by the remarkable usage which Paul makes of the passage in II Corinthians 4:6a.[38] In the second place, that which God speaks brings his will to pass. It is powerful and efficacious. "For he spake and it was *done*; he commanded, and it stood fast" (Psalm 33:9); "Through faith we understand that the worlds were framed by the word of God" (Hebrews 11:3a). These passages teach that the Word of God is efficacious.[39]

van het begin der wereld aan in mensentaal gesproken en gezegd wat Hij te zeggen had in de taal, welker vorming hij blijkens Genesis 2:19 opzettelijk aan de mens had overgelaten".

[37] With respect to the words "and God saw", Keil comments that it "is not an anthropomorphism at variance with enlightened thoughts of God; for man's seeing has its type in God's, and God's seeing is not a mere expression of delight of the eye or of pleasure in His work, but is of the deepest significance to every created thing, being the seal of the perfection which God has impressed upon it, and by which its continuance before God and through God is determined" (*Biblical Commentary on the Old Testament*, Grand Rapids, 1949, Vol. I, p. 50).

[38] According to Paul, the content of God's speaking (ὁ εἰπών) is found in the words ἐκ σκότους φῶς λάμψει. In this remarkable utterance Paul also emphasizes the distinction between light and darkness. Perhaps a reflection of the truth that God spoke is found on the Shabaka stone, in which Atum's coming into being is attributed to the heart and tongue of Ptah. Cf. James Pritchard: *Ancient Near Eastern Texts*, Princeton, 1950, p. 5a.

[39] Cf. also Deut. 8:3; I Kg. 8:56; Ps. 105:8; 119:50; 147:15; Isa. 45:23; 55:11 ff.; Matt. 24:35; Lk. 4:32; 24:19; Heb. 4:12; I Pet. 1:23; II Pet. 3:5. In these passages it is well to note the connection between word and deed. The word is powerful and accomplishes the purpose for which it was spoken. It is also necessary, however, to note that there is no power re-

Hence, whatever be the term that we employ to characterize such a phrase as "and God said", we must insist that the phrase represents an effectual divine activity which may very properly be denominated "speaking".[40]

It is necessary, however, to examine the extent of "anthropomorphism" in the passages adduced by Professor Ridderbos. If the term "anthropomorphic" may legitimately be used at all, we would say that whereas it might apply to some elements of Genesis 2:7, it does not include all of them. In other words, if anthropomorphism is present, it is not present in each element of the verse. The words "and God breathed" may be termed anthropomorphic,[41] but that is the extent to which the term may be employed. The man was real, the dust was real, the ground was real as was also the breath of life. To these elements of the verse the term "anthropomorphism" cannot legitimately be applied. Nor can everything in Genesis 3:21 be labeled with the term "anthropomorphic". We need but think, for example, of the man and the woman and the coats of skin.

What, then, shall we say about the representation of the first chapter of Genesis that God created the heaven and

siding in the word conceived as an independent entity divorced from God. God's Word is powerful because God himself gives power to it, and brings to pass what he has promised. If the same "Word" were spoken by anyone other than God, it would not accomplish what it does when spoken by him.

[40] At the same time we cannot state specifically what this speaking of God is. There is an infinite difference between God's speaking and man's. Although both may legitimately be designated "speaking", yet they cannot be identified, for man as a finite being speaks as a creature; the speaking of God on the other hand is that of an infinite being.

[41] The phrase "and God formed" is not merely figurative and devoid of meaning. Although with physical hands God did not form the body of Adam, nevertheless, God did produce Adam's body from the dust in such a way that his action may accurately be designated a "forming".

Even the words "and God breathed" indicate a definite action on God's part. The divine breathing was not accomplished by means of physical, material organs. It was a divine, not a human, breathing. Although the term "anthropomorphic" may be applied to the phrase "and God breathed", nevertheless, the phrase is not empty of content. This is true, even though one cannot state precisely what the divine breathing was. Cf. Visée, op. cit., pp. 636 f.

the earth in six days? Is this anthropomorphic language? We would answer this question in the negative, for the word anthropomorphic, if it is a legitimate word at all, can be applied to God alone and cannot properly be used of the six days. In speaking of six days Moses may conceivably have been employing figurative, literal, or poetical language, but it was not anthropomorphic. Hence, we do not believe that it is accurate to speak of the six days as an anthropomorphic mode of expression.

From the presence of "anthropomorphic" words or expressions in Genesis one, it does not follow that the mention of the days is anthropomorphic nor does it follow that the days are to be understood in a topical or non-chronological order rather than chronologically. If the days are to be interpreted non-chronologically, the evidence for this must be something other than the presence of anthropomorphisms in the first chapter of Genesis. The occurrence of anthropomorphic language in Genesis one in itself, if such language really does occur, sheds no light one way or another upon the question whether the days are to be understood topically or chronologically. For that matter even the presence of figurative language or of a schematic arrangement, taken by themselves, would not warrant the conclusion that the days were not chronological.

2. The Appeal to Genesis 2:5

One of the strongest arguments in favor of a nonchronological order of the days is thought to be found in an appeal to Genesis 2:5.[42] The presupposition of this verse, it is held, is that during the period of creation divine providence was in operation "through processes which any reader would recognize as normal in the natural world of his day".[43] If in Genesis 2:5 ff. there is embedded the principle that God's providence during the creation period operated in the same manner as it does at the present time, then the view that the days of Genesis one were twenty-four hours in length would

---

[42] Kline: *op. cit.*, pp. 146–157.
[43] *Op. cit.*, p. 150.

scarcely be tenable. For, to take an example, if the third day began with an earth covered with water and then in the course of that day dry land emerged, the evaporation would have to take place at such a rate of speed that it would not be the normal ordinary working of divine providence. Even if the days be regarded as longer than twenty-four hours, so the argument runs, difficulty appears, for then we must hold that there was vegetation without the sun.

The question to be considered is whether upon the basis of Genesis 2:5 we are justified in believing that the method in which divine providence operated during the creation period was the same as that in effect at present. To answer this question it is necessary to consider briefly the relation of Genesis 1 and 2. In the first place Genesis two is not, nor does it profess to be, a second account of creation.[44] Although it does mention creative acts, it is a sequel to the creation narrative of Genesis one and a preparation for the history of the fall contained in chapter 3. This is proved by the phrase "These are the generations of the heavens and the earth" (Gen. 2:4a).

To understand the significance of this phrase we must note the word תּוֹלְדוֹת which is obviously derived from יָלַד, "to bear", and in the Hiph'il stem with which it is related, the meaning is "to beget". The תּוֹלְדוֹת therefore are "those things which are begotten", and Genesis 2:4a should then be translated literally, "These are the things begotten of heaven and earth". The section of Genesis beginning with 2:4 is an

---

44 This statement is made in the light of the constant affirmations to the contrary. Thus, Ralph H. Elliott: *op. cit.*, p. 28 speaks of "The First or Priestly Account of Creation (1:1 to 2:4a)" and "The Second Creation Account (2:4b–25)" (p. 41). Perhaps it is an encouraging sign that von Rad labels 2:4b–25 "Die jahwistische Geschichte von Paradies" (*Das erste Buch Mose*, Göttingen, 1953, p. 58). The English translation renders "The Yahwistic Story of Paradise" (*Genesis*, Philadelphia, MCMLXI, translated by John H. Marks, p. 71). On the other hand the following comment of von Rad is very disappointing, "Die kosmologischen Vorstellungen, von denen unser jahwistischer Schöpfungsbericht ausgeht, sind also sehr verschieden von denen, die uns bei P. begegnet sind und müssen aus einem ganz anderen Überlieferungskreis stammen" (*op. cit.*, p. 61). Once, however, we abandon the untenable documentary hypothesis and recognize the true nature of Genesis, we can understand the proper relationship between the first and second chapters.

account of those things which are begotten of heaven and earth. This is not to say that it is silent on the subject of the heaven and earth themselves, but it is not an account of their origin.[45] It deals rather with what was begotten of them, namely, man, whose body is of the earth and whose soul is of heavenly origin, inbreathed by God himself.[46]

It is necessary to examine more closely the usage of this phrase in Genesis. Genesis is divided into two great sections: I. The Creation of Heaven and Earth, and II. The Generations. The second section is again subdivided into ten sections each being introduced with the word תּוֹלְדוֹת. In each case this word indicates the result or product, that which is produced. With the genitive, however, in this case "the heavens and the earth", Moses refers to a point of beginning.[47] In Genesis 11:27, for example, we read, "these are the generations of Terah". This does not mean that we are now introduced to an account of Terah; rather, the account of Terah is completed. There may, indeed, be certain statements about Terah to follow, but the section before us is concerned with an account of those begotten of Terah, in this case, Abraham.

Genesis 2:4 in effect declares that the account of the creation

---

[45] Skinner (*The International Critical Commentary, Genesis*, New York, 1925, p. 40) states that it is doubtful whether the word תּוֹלְדוֹת can bear the meaning "origin". Driver (*The Book of Genesis*, London, 1926, p. 19) asserts that "generations" is applied metaphorically to "heaven and earth" and denotes the things which "*might be regarded metaphorically as proceeding from them, . . . i. e.*, just the contents of ch. 1". Such, however, is not the force of the phrase.

It is practically an axiom of modern negative criticism that 2:4a belongs to the so-called P document. What follows, however, is said to be JE. Hence, it is claimed, 2:4a cannot be a superscription to 2:4b ff. Von Rad (*op. cit.*, p. 49) candidly acknowledges this. But why may not Moses have employed previously existing documents and himself have united them by means of the phrase אֵלֶּה תוֹלְדוֹת? Is there any reason why 2:4a cannot serve as a superscription to the second section of Genesis? Why in the interests of a supposed diversity of documents destroy a fundamental unity as clear-cut and beautiful as that which underlies the structure of Genesis?

[46] *Cf.* William Henry Green: *The Unity of the Book of Genesis*, New York, 1895, pp. 7–20.

[47] This phrase has been most competently discussed in recent times by B. Holwerda: *Dictaten*, Deel I, *Historia Revelationis Veteris Testamenti*, Eerste Aflevering, Kampen, 1954, pp. 9–17.

of heaven and earth is completed, and that the author is now going to focus his attention upon what was begotten of heaven and earth, namely, man. It is in the light of this fact that Genesis 2:5 is to be understood. The primary reference of this verse is to man, not to the creation, and the purpose of chapter 2 is to manifest the goodness of God in giving to man a paradise for his earthly dwelling. "The earth is the Lord's and the fulness thereof, the world and they that dwell therein" (Ps. 24:1). Although the earth is the Lord's and although he might cause man to dwell on it where he would, nevertheless he prepared a wondrous garden for his guest. To emphasize the beauty of the garden, but above all the goodness of God, a contrast is introduced. Man is to dwell as God's guest not in a waterless waste, but in a planted garden. The waterless ground of Genesis 2:5 stands in contrast to the well-watered Paradise which is to be man's earthly home.[48]

Two reasons are given why plants had not yet grown. On the one hand it had not rained, and on the other there was no man to till the ground. The garden cannot be planted until the ground has been watered, nor can it be tended until man is on hand. Both of these reasons, therefore, look forward to man's home, the garden, and to the one who is to inhabit that garden. At this point, however, an exegetical question arises. Does Genesis 2:5 intend to state that the entire earth was barren, or is its purpose rather to show that in contrast to a waterless waste, the abode of man was to be a garden? Perhaps this question cannot be settled entirely, and it is the part of wisdom not be dogmatic, although the latter alternative has much to commend it.[49]

[48] The theme of refreshing waters is carried throughout Scripture. In particular we may note Exodus 17:6; Ps. 65:9; Prov. 21:1; Isa. 12:3; 32:2; Jn. 4:10 ff., 7:38; Rev. 21:6; 22:1, 17. Visée makes a pertinent comment (*loc. cit.*, p. 638), "Genoemde gegevens weerspreken elke gedachte als zou het in deze hoofdstukken verhaalde passen in een, primitief milieu, een door de cultuur nog niet opengelegd en onontslaten gebied". T. C. Mitchell ("Archaeology and Genesis I–XI", *Faith and Thought*, Vol. 91, No. 1, Summer 1959, pp. 28–49) gives an interesting discussion of this question.

[49] Some commentators assume that the reference is to the entire earth. Procksch, however (*Die Genesis übersetzt und erklärt*, Leipzig, 1913, p. 21), states that "das Weltbild ist hier dem Steppenlande entnommen". שָׂדֶה is "not 'the widespread plain of the earth, the broad expanse of land,'

Whichever of these positions we adopt, we may note that the fulfillment of at least one of the two requirements necessary for plant growth could have been accomplished by ordinary providence. If, as is sometimes held, the watering of the ground was the work of subterranean waters,[50] did they water

but a field of arable land, soil fit for cultivation which forms only a part of the 'earth' or 'ground.' " "The creation of the plants is not alluded to here at all, but simply the planting of the garden in Eden" (Keil: *op. cit.*, p. 77). "All the faces of the ground" is also said to be a phrase which "ist auch hier nicht die gesamte Erdflache (אֶרֶץ), sondern nur das anbaufähige Erdreich" (Procksch: *op. cit.*, p. 22).

[50] The various interpretations of אֵד may be found in Kline: *op. cit.*, p. 150. König (*Die Genesis eingeleitet, übersetzt und erklärt*, Gütersloh, 1925, pp. 198–200) is one of the strongest defenders of the view that אֵד means mist (Dunst), for he thinks that the rising of a mist is a natural preparation for rainfall. "Denn selbstverständlich ist gemeint, dass der aufsteigende Wasserdunst sich wieder als Regen gesenkt habe" (p. 199). König thinks that it is a wrong method to derive the meaning of a Hebrew word directly from the Babylonian. *edu*, therefore, is not to determine the meaning of אֵד. Aalders (*op. cit.*, p. 114) also adopts this position. He asserts that the mist (damp) arose from the earth, which could hardly be said of a flood. In Job 36:27 the meaning "flood" is thought not to be suitable. In the formation of the rain clouds, says Aalders, despite the difficulties of Job 36:27, "mist" is understandable, but not "flood".

It should be noted, however, that none of the ancient versions rendered this word as "mist". Thus, LXX, πηγή; Aquila, ἐπιβλυσμός; Vulgate, fons; Syriac ܡܒܘܥܐ. What really rules out the rendering "rain" or "mist" is the verb וְהִשְׁקָה. The causing of the earth to drink is the work of the אֵד which arises from the ground. Obviously, a mist which arises may moisten the ground, but how can it, inasmuch as it comes up *from* the earth, cause the earth to drink? The translation "mist" must be abandoned. Albright's suggestion ("The Predeuteronomic Primeval", *Journal of Biblical Literature*, Vol. 58, 1939, p. 102) that the word אֵד be traced to the Id, the subterranean source of fresh water, has much to commend it. All mythological or polytheistic associations, however, are completely missing in Genesis 2:5. In support of Albright's position appeal may be made to Samuel N. Kramer: *Enki and Ninḥursag*, New Haven, 1945, p. 13, lines 45, 46, " 'mouth whence issues the water of the earth,' bring thee sweet water from the earth". Even if we adopt the view that אֵד means "mist" or "cloud" and that the reference is to a mist which arises from the ground and returns to water it in the form of rain, that does not prove that ordinary providential activity prevailed on the third day. On the third day there were two works, and both were creative works, namely:

1. FIAT — FULFILLMENT (Gathering of the waters into one place and appearance of the dry land).
2. FIAT — FULFILLMENT (Earth sending forth grass, etc.).

If Genesis 2:6 is to be fitted in here, it obviously must fall between the

the entire surface of the globe? If they did, then such a work, while not the method that God today employs to water the whole earth, nevertheless may have been a providential work. To water the ground, therefore, may have been accomplished by a *modus operandi* similar to that by which God today works in his providential activity. Nevertheless, it was a unique act, and one never to be repeated. If it was a providential work, it was unique and distinct, for God has never again watered the entire earth in this manner. If, on the other hand, the אֲדָמָה here has a somewhat restricted sense, as is probably the case, then we certainly cannot in any sense appeal to this verse for help in the interpretation of Genesis one, for in this case the verse merely emphasizes that the paradise was planted in what once was wasteland.[51]

In the second place, the fulfillment of the need for man to cultivate the garden was not met by means of ordinary providential working. To meet this need there was special supernatural activity, namely, the divine forming and the divine inbreathing.[52]

What relationship, then, does Genesis 2:5 ff. sustain to the third day of creation mentioned in Genesis one? If Genesis

first and second fiat. Activity by means of "fiat" creation however, is not the *modus operandi* of divine providence. If, therefore, divine providential activity was introduced after the accomplishment of the first fiat, it was interrupted again by the second fiat and its fulfillment. Even, therefore, if Genesis 2:5 ff. could be made to show that divine providence was present during the third day, what is stated of the third day in Genesis 1 makes it clear that divine providence *did not prevail* during the third day.

[51] It is well to note the distinction between אֲדָמָה and אֶרֶץ which is found in this section. Whereas אֶרֶץ refers to the earth generally, אֲדָמָה is the ground upon which man dwells. The אֲדָמָה is more restricted in reference than אֶרֶץ, and it is also that ground which produces the sustenance that will sustain the life of אָדָם and which אָדָם must cultivate. Procksch comments, "אָדָם und אֲדָמָה sind aufeinander angewiesen, der Mensch ist dem Wesen nach Bauer" (*op. cit.*, p. 22), but such a conclusion does not necessarily follow.

[52] In the following comment Gunkel presses the language of Scripture in an unwarrantable manner: "Diese Zeit weiss noch nichts von dem Supernaturalismus der späteren Epoche, sondern sie erzählt unbefangen, dass „Gott Jahve" seine Geschöpfe „formte", d.h. sie mit seinen eigenen Händen bildete, wie der Töpfer den Ton knetet" (*Die Urgeschichte und die Patriarchen*, Göttingen, 1921 (Die Schriften des Alten Testaments, 1/1, p. 55)).

2:5 has reference to the entire globe, it applies to the third day and merely describes the "dry land" of the third day. But if that be the case, the verse does not show that the present *modus operandi* of divine providence, while it may have been present, necessarily *prevailed* on the third day. At the most it teaches that God watered the ground by means of an אֵד that kept rising from the earth.[53] If, on the other hand, Genesis 2:5 ff. simply describes the preparation of the garden of Eden, it may not be applicable at all to the third day, but may rather be fitted into the sixth day. While there are difficulties in the interpretation of the verse, it is clear that it cannot be used to establish the thesis that the present *modus operandi* of divine providence *prevailed* during the third day. At most it shows that such a mode may have been present.

The appeal to Genesis 2:5a, it must be remembered, to establish the thesis that during the days of creation the *modus operandi* of divine providence was the same as is at present in effect, can only have validity if it proves that there was no supernatural intrusion such as might be found, for example, in the working of miracles. But such supernatural intrusion was certainly present in the creation of man (Gen. 2:7). And the only works ascribed to the third day are creative works, not those of ordinary divine providence. Indeed, on no viewpoint can it be established that ordinary providential working *prevailed* on the third day. The only works assigned to this day were the result of special, divine, creative fiats. If ordinary providence existed during the third day, it was

[53] The force of יַעֲלֶה must be noted. Delitzsch takes it as indicating a single action "normirt durch den historischen Zusammenh. in Imperfectbedeutung" (*Commentar über die Genesis*, Leipzig, 1860, p. 140). Tuch, however (*Commentar über die Genesis*, Halle, 1871, p. 52) takes the verb as in verse 10, and Isa. 6:4 "von der werdenden, allmälig erst geschehenden Handlung". The latter is a more accurate representation of the Hebrew. Driver believes that the imperfect has frequentative force, "used to go up" (*A Treatise on the Use of the Tenses in Hebrew*, Oxford, MDCCCXCII, p. 128). Gesenius, Kautzsch, Cowley state that the imperfect here expresses an action which continued throughout a longer or shorter period, "*a mist went up*, continually" (*Gesenius' Hebrew Grammar*, Oxford, 1910, p. 314). William Henry Green (*A Grammar of the Hebrew Language*, New York, 1891, p. 313) also renders *used to go up*, "not only at the moment of time previously referred to but from that time onward".

interrupted at two points by divine fiats. Even apart from any consideration of Genesis 2:5, therefore, it cannot be held that the present *modus operandi* of divine providence *prevailed* on the third day, nor does the appeal to Genesis 2:5 prove such a thing. On the contrary, all that is stated of the third day (Gen. 1:9–15) shows that the works of that day were creative works and not those of ordinary providence. An appeal to Genesis 2:5 therefore does not support the position that the days are to be taken in a non-chronological manner.[54]

3. The Schematic Nature of Genesis One

A further argument adduced to support the non-chronological view is found in the claim that Genesis one is schematic in nature. Thus, the author is said to divide the vegetable world into two groups, plants which give seed by means of the fruits and plants which give seed in a more direct way. In verses 24 ff. something of the same nature is said to be found.[55]

It may very well be that the author of Genesis one has arranged his material in a schematic manner. On this particular question we shall have more to say when presenting a positive interpretation of the chapter. At this point, however, one or two remarks will suffice. In the first place, from the fact that some of the material in Genesis one is given in schematic form, it does not necessarily follow that what is stated is to be dismissed as figurative or as not describing what actually occurred. Sometimes a schematic arrangement may serve the purpose of emphasis. Whether the language is figurative or symbolical, however, must be determined upon exegetical grounds. Secondly, a schematic disposition of the material in Genesis one does not prove, nor does it even

---

[54] Even if אֵד referred to evaporation (and as shown in note 31 this is not possible) it is difficult to understand how it could have provided rainfall sufficient for the entire earth. And if the reference is local, how can evaporation have arisen from a land in which there had been no rain or dew, and how on this interpretation can Genesis 2:5 be fitted into the third day of Genesis 1? These considerations support the view that the אֵד designates subterranean waters, waters which may have entered the earth when the division between seas and dry land was made.

[55] *Quarterly*, p. 223.

suggest, that the days are to be taken in a non-chronological sense. There appears to be a certain schematization, for example, in the genealogies of Matthew one, but it does not follow that the names of the genealogies are to be understood in a non-chronological sense, or that Matthew teaches that the generations from Abraham to David parallel, or were contemporary with, those from David to the Babylonian captivity and that these in turn are parallel to the generations from the Babylonian captivity to Christ.[56] Matthew, in other words, even though he has adopted a certain schematic arrangement, namely, fourteen generations to each group, is not presenting three different aspects of the same thing. He is not saying the same thing in three different ways. He has a schematic arrangement, but that does not mean that he has thrown chronology to the winds. Why, then, must we conclude that, merely because of a schematic arrangement, Moses has disposed of chronology?

4. Is the First-Hand Impression of Genesis One Correct?

In defense of the non-chronological view of the days it is asserted, and rightly, that Genesis one is not the product of a naive writer.[57] At the same time, so it is argued, if we read Genesis "without prepossession or suspicion" we receive the impression that the author meant to teach a creation in six ordinary days and, more than that, to teach that the earth was created before the sun, moon and stars. This impression, apparently, is to be considered naive. "Is it good", asks Ridderbos, "to read Genesis one thus simply, 'avec des yeux ingenus'?"[58] It is, of course, true that the first-hand impression that comes to us upon reading certain passages of the Bible may not be the correct one. Further reflection may lead to a re-evaluation of our first-hand impression and to the adoption of a different interpretation. But if we label a first-hand

---

[56] Cf. Matthew 1:1–17. Verse 17 gives a summary comment. It would certainly be unwarranted to conclude that, merely because of the schematic arrangement in Matthew, the names were to be interpreted figuratively or symbolically.

[57] Conflict, p. 29.

[58] Ibid., p. 29.

impression naive, we cannot do so merely upon the basis of our own independent and "autonomous" opinion as to what is naive. Only exegesis can tell us whether a certain impression is or is not naive. We ourselves, upon the basis of our subjective judgment, are not warranted in making such a pronouncement. If the first-hand impression that any Scripture makes upon us is naive, it is Scripture alone that can enable us so to judge, and not we ourselves apart from the Scripture.

If we understand it correctly, the argument now before us is that the *prima facie* impression which we receive from Genesis one is naive, and not to be accepted.[59] This consideration raises the question why it is naive to believe that God created all things in six ordinary days or that the earth was created before the sun? This line of argumentation would prove too much, for it could be applied to other passages of Scripture as well. One who reads the Gospels, for example, is likely to receive the impression that they teach that Jesus rose from the dead. But can we in this day of science seriously be expected to believe that such an event really took place? At the same time, the Gospels can hardly be called the products of naive writers. Are we, therefore, able to understand the writers' meaning at first glance? Do the writers really intend to teach that Jesus rose from the dead or may they not be employing this particular manner of statement to express some great truth?

Only solid exegesis can lead to the true understanding of Scripture. If, in any instance, what appears to be the *prima*

---

[59] At this point Ridderbos quotes the well-known statement of von Rad, a statement which he thinks "is of importance here" (*Conflict*, p. 29), namely, " 'It is doctrine which has been cautiously enriched in a process of very slow, century-long growth' " ("es ist Lehre, die in langsamstem, jahrehundertelangem Wachstum sich behutsam angereichert hat" (von Rad, *op. cit.*, p. 36). In the sense intended by von Rad, however, this statement cannot be accepted, for there is no evidence to support it. If Moses had before him written documents which he employed in compiling Genesis 1, these documents simply reflected an original revelation concerning the creation. When Moses as an inspired penman wrote, he was superintended by God's Spirit, so that he wrote precisely what God wished him to write. The form and content of Genesis 1 were the work of Moses writing under the inspiration of God's Spirit, and the words of Genesis 1 are God-breathed words (*cf.* II Tim. 3:16).

facie meaning is not the true one, it is exegesis alone, and not our independent judgment that the apparent *prima facie* meaning is naive, that will bring us to the truth.

5. The Author of Genesis had a Sublime Concept of God

Somewhat similar is the argument that inasmuch as the author has such a sublime concept of God, we cannot believe that he meant to say that God used a day for each of his great works.[60] The same objection must be raised against this type of reasoning as was urged against the idea that some of the representations in Genesis one are naive. It is not the prerogative of the exegete on his own to determine what a sublime conception of God is.

It might also be remarked in this connection that if the idea of creation in six days really does detract from a sublime concept of God, the author of Genesis was certainly ill-advised in using it. If the author really possessed this sublime concept, why did he employ a scheme which would detract from that concept? Would it not have been better if he had simply told us the truth about creation in a straightforward manner, rather than used a scheme which presents a way of creation inconsistent with a sublime concept of God?

6. Parallelism of the Days

In favor of a non-chronological order of the days, it is also argued that there exists a certain parallelism between the first three and the last three days. Thus, it is held, the six days are divided into two groups of three each. The parallelism is thought to be seen in the light of the first day and the light-bearers of the fourth.[61] Again, on the second day the firmament is created which divides the waters above and below it, and on the fifth day the waters are filled with living creatures. On the third day dry land appears, and on the sixth the inhabitants of earth are created.

[60] *Conflict*, p. 31. "Are we really to take literally the representation that for every great work (or two works) of creation He used a day?"
[61] *Quarterly*, p. 223.

Assuming that such parallelism actually exists, at best it proves that days four, five and six parallel days one, two and three. Even on this construction, however, a certain amount of chronology is retained. Days two-five must follow days one-four, and days three-six must follow days two-five. Hence, even here there would be chronological order, namely, days one-four, two-five, three-six.

As soon as one examines the text carefully, however, it becomes apparent that such a simple arrangement is not actually present. We may note that the light-bearers of the fourth day are placed in the firmament of heaven (1:14, 17). The firmament, however, was made on the second day (1:6, 7). Inasmuch as the fourth day is said to parallel the first, it follows that the work of the second day (making the firmament) must precede that of the first and fourth days (*i. e.*, placing the light-bearers in the firmament). If the first and fourth days are really parallel in the sense that they present two aspects of the same thing, and if part of the work of the fourth day is the placing of the luminaries in the firmament, it follows that the firmament must be present to receive the luminaries. The firmament therefore, existed not only before the fourth day, but, inasmuch as it is a parallel to the fourth, before the first day also. This is an impossible conclusion, for verse three is connected with verse two grammatically, in that the three circumstantial clauses of verse two modify the main verb of verse three. At the same time by its use of the introductory words וְהָאָרֶץ, verse two clearly introduces the detailed account of which a general statement is given in verse one. Verse two is the beginning of the section or unit, the first action of which is expressed by the main verb of verse three.[62] To hold that days two-five precede days one-four is simply to abandon all grammatical considerations.

Furthermore, if day five is a parallel to day two, and day two is earlier than days one-four Genesis one is practically reduced to nonsense. On the fifth day the birds fly in the open firmament of heaven, and the fish fill the seas. This may cause no difficulty as far as the fish are concerned, but

---

[62] *Cf.* "The Relation of the First Verse of Genesis One to Verses Two and Three", *Westminster Theological Journal*, Vol. XXI, No. 2 (May 1959), pp. 133–146.

light has not yet been created, and light is a prerequisite for the life of birds. A further difficulty also emerges. The fish are to swim in the seas (יַמִּים), but the seas were not formed until the third day. Day five, it must be noted, does not refer to the primeval ocean, but to the seas. From these brief considerations it is apparent that we cannot regard Genesis one as containing two groups of three days, each day of one group being a genuine parallel to the corresponding day of the other set.

It is now in place to ask in how far there actually does exist parallelism between two groups of three days each. That there is a certain amount of parallelism cannot be denied. The light of day one and the light-bearers of day four may be said to sustain a relationship to one another, but they are not identical. They are not two aspects of the same thing. The light of day one is called "day" (יוֹם) and the heavenly bodies of day four are made to rule the day. That which rules (the heavenly bodies) and that which is ruled (the day) are not the same. In the very nature of the case they must be distinguished. The production of each is introduced by the short יְהִי ("let there be"). At this point, however, the correspondence ceases.

Even though there may be a certain parallelism between the mention of light on day one and the light-bearers of day four, it is but a parallelism in that light and light-bearers bear a relationship one to another. What is stated about the light and the light-bearers, however, is quite different. The creation of light is the result of God's fiat. God himself then divides between the light and the darkness. On the fourth day God makes the light-bearers. Unlike the light of day one, they do not spring into existence at his creative word.

It must also be noted that the functions of the light and those of the light-bearers are not parallel. In fact, no function whatever is given for the light of day one.[63] On the other hand, the light-bearers of day four are brought into existence for the purpose of serving a world in which dry land and seas have been separated, a world on which plant and animal life

---

[63] It is true that God calls the light "day", but no statement of function is made such as is found in connection with the sun and moon.

can exist. The division between light and darkness which God made on day one was at a time when the world was covered with water, and there was no firmament.[64] The light-bearers, on the other hand, were placed in the firmament of heaven, a firmament that was brought into existence only on the second day. It is obvious, then, that the work of day one and that of day four are two distinct and different works. They do not parallel one another, other than that light characterizes one day and light-bearers the other.

Do the second and fifth days parallel one another? On day two there is a twofold fiat ("let there be a firmament . . . and let it divide") and the fulfillment consists of two acts of God ("God made . . . divided"), followed by a further act ("God called"). On the fifth day there is also a twofold fiat ("let the waters bring forth . . . and the fowl let it fly") and then comes a fulfillment consisting of a threefold creative act of God ("God created . . . great whales . . . every living thing . . . every winged fowl") and this is followed by two additional acts of God ("God saw . . . God blessed"). As far as form is concerned, the parallelism is by no means exact.

Nor is there exact parallelism in content. The swarming waters and their inhabitants which were created in the fifth day are not to be identified with the primeval waters of day two. Rather, it is expressly stated that the fish are to fill the waters in the seas (verse 22), and the seas were brought into existence on the third day.[65] For that matter, if a mere parallel with water is sought, we may note that "the waters" and the "abyss" are mentioned in verse two also.

The birds are created that they may fly above the earth upon the faces of the expanse of heaven (verse 20). Is this a parallel to the work of day two? Actually the only parallel consists in the mention of the word "firmament". Now, it is true that the birds fly in the firmament, but they also belong

[64] Although it is not explicitly stated in verse 2 that the earth was covered with water, this seems to be implied, and the fiat of verse 9 shows that such was the case. *Cf.* "The Interpretation of Genesis 1:2", *Westminster Theological Journal*, Vol. XXIII, No. 2 (May 1961), p. 171.

[65] Ridderbos says that this must not be given much weight (*Conflict*, p. 35). It is sufficiently weighty, however, to show that the alleged parallelism between days two and five is an illusion.

to the earth. They are created first of all to fly above the earth (עַל הָאָרֶץ) and are commanded to multiply in the earth (וְהָעוֹף יָרֶב בָּאָרֶץ). The sphere in which the birds are to live is explicitly said to be the earth, not the firmament; and the earth, capable of sustaining bird life, did not appear until the third day. In the light of these emphases it is difficult to understand how a parallel between days two and five is present. Let us briefly examine the relationship between the third and sixth days. There are three fiats on the third day (waters . . . dry land . . . earth). The first two are followed by a threefold act of God ("God called . . . called he . . . God saw") and the third fiat is followed by a twofold act ("the earth brought forth . . . God saw"). On the sixth day, following the fiat and fulfillment with respect to the living creatures, a unique method of statement is introduced, which has no parallel in the description of the third day. Indeed, it is difficult to discover any parallel of thought with the third day. At best it may be said that the dry land of day three is the sphere in which man and the animals live. This, however, is a parallelism which applies only to a part of the third day.

A word must be said about the view that days one, two and three present the realm and days four, five and six the ruler in that realm, and that therefore there are two parallel trios of days.[66] With respect to days one and three we may remark that light is not the sphere in which the light-bearers rule. The sphere of the primitive light, however, is the day. "God called the light day." On day four the sphere in which the light-bearers rule is the day and night to give light upon the earth. It is true that they are placed in the expanse of heaven, but this is in order that they may give light upon the earth.

The sphere of the sea creatures of day five is not the firmament of day two but the seas (verse 22) of the earth, and the sphere in which the birds rule is also the earth (verse 22).

---

[66] This view was set forth by V. Zapletal: *Der Schöpfungsbericht*, Freiburg, 1902. Zapletal rejects what he calls the scholastic distinction of "opus distinctionis et opus ornatus", a distinction which, he claims, is influenced by the Vulgate translation of 2:1 "et omnis ornatus eorum". Instead, he would emphasize the Hebrew צָבָא and speak of "die Schöpfung der Heere (ṣābhā)" and "die Schöpfung der Regionen, der Kampfplätze dieser Heere," *i. e.*, "productio regionum et exercituum" (p. 72).

The same is true of the land animals and man; the spheres in which they rule is not merely the dry land of day three, but the entire earth, including the fish of the sea, which God has prepared for them. The matter may be set forth in tabular form as follows:

	RULER	REALM
day four	light-bearers	the earth
day five	sea creatures	seas of earth
	winged fowl	earth
day six	land animals	earth
	man	earth

Thus, the view that days one, two and three present the realm and days four, five and six the ruler in that realm, is contrary to the explicit statements of Genesis.

7. The Historiography of Genesis One

The historiography of the Bible, it is said, is not quite the same as modern historiography.[67] Genesis one is thought to contain a peculiar sort of history, for man is not present to play a role alongside of God. Often, it is argued, the biblical writers group their facts together in an artificial manner and deviate from a chronological order, without any indication of the fact being given. Indeed, without warning, the biblical writer may deviate from a chronological order and arrange his material artificially.

Ridderbos has aptly called attention, for example, to Genesis two as a passage in which a certain schematic arrangement is present and he rightly points out that Genesis two is an

---

[67] *Quarterly*, p. 225; *Conflict*, p. 30. Visée (*op. cit.*, p. 636) does not wish to apply the word "history" to Genesis 1, inasmuch as he thinks it is not a suitable word to use ("niet juist"). Nevertheless, his comments are true to Scripture. He regards Genesis 1 as a factual account of what actually took place, but withholds from it the term "history" because it is not an eyewitness account or the fruit of historical investigation. There can be no serious objection to this position, although we prefer to apply the term history to all that has happened, even though our knowledge thereof should come to us through special divine revelation (*e. g.*, Genesis 1) instead of by historical investigation.

We do not see what is gained, however, by labelling Genesis 1, *Verbondsgeschiedenis* (Popma, *op. cit.*, p. 622). Genesis 1 is the divine revelation of the creation. That point must be insisted upon.

74

introduction to the account of the fall of man.[68] Genesis two
may well serve as an example of a passage of Scripture in
which chronological considerations are not paramount. This
will be apparent if we simply list certain matters mentioned
in the chapter.

1. God formed man (verse 7).
2. God planted a garden (verse 8a).
3. God placed the man in the garden (verse 8b).
4. God caused the trees to grow (verse 9a).
5. God placed the man in the garden (verse 15a).

It is obvious that a chronological order is not intended here.
How many times did God place man in the garden? What did
God do with man before he placed him in the garden? How
many times did God plant the garden, or did God first plant
a garden and then later plant the trees? Clearly enough Moses
here has some purpose other than that of chronology in mind.

In chapter two events are narrated from the standpoint
of emphasis, in preparation for the account of the fall.[69]
Looked at from this viewpoint, the chapter is remarkably
rich in meaning. First of all we may note that it is not a
duplicate or second account of creation. Hence, we should
not make the mistake of trying to force its "order of events"
into harmony with the order of events given in chapter one.

The section begins by giving us a barren earth, for there
had been no rain and there was no man to till the ground.
God, however, did not desire man to dwell in a barren earth
but in a garden, for man was to be God's guest on this earth.
Hence, God will prepare a dwelling place for him. First the
ground is watered and then man is created. For man the
garden is made, God's garden, and man is placed therein.
The garden, however, is a place of exquisite beauty, and trees
are made to grow therein. Thus we are prepared for the
prohibition not to eat of the fruit of the tree of the knowledge
of good and evil. Further information about the location of
the garden and its well-watered character is then given, that
we may learn that its trees will truly thrive. There, in a place
of great charm, man is placed as God's servant to work the

[68] *Op. cit.*, pp. 26 f.
[69] *Cf.* W. H. Green: *The Unity of the Book of Genesis*, New York, 1895,
pp. 7–36, for an excellent discussion of the nature of Genesis 2.

garden. The garden is not Adam's but God's, and God alone may prescribe the manner in which Adam is to live therein. Adam is forbidden to partake of the tree of the knowledge of good and evil.

When this important matter is disposed of, Moses then introduces a question that has to do with man's relation to his environment. His relation to God, however, must first be made clear (verses 16, 17) and then that to his environment. He is not to live alone, but is to have the animals as his helpers. Yet they are not sufficient to correspond to him; only the woman can be such a help. Her creation is then related, and Adam recognizes her who was to show herself a hindrance as a help that is essentially one with himself. One final point must be mentioned to prepare for the account of the fall. Adam and Eve were naked, yet not ashamed. They were good, and no evil was found in them.

What Moses does in Genesis two is truly remarkable. He emphasizes just those points which need to be stressed, in order that the reader may be properly prepared to understand the account of the fall.[70] Are we, however, warranted in assuming that, inasmuch as the material in Genesis two is arranged in a non-chronological manner, the same is likely to be true of Genesis one? It is true that in Genesis one man is not present until the sixth day, but is this sufficient warrant for claiming that the days are to be taken in a non-chronological manner?

In the very nature of the case Genesis one is *sui generis*. Its content could have been known only by special communication from God. Obviously, it is not a history of mankind, but it is the divine revelation of the creation of heaven and earth and of man, and it is to be interpreted only upon the basis of serious exegesis. The fact that Genesis two discusses its subject in a partly non-chronological manner really has

---

[70] "This phenomenon (*i. e.*, that in prophetic and apocalyptic writings "events are telescoped, grouped, and arranged in a given manner") should make us hospitable toward the idea that in Genesis 1, which treats not the distant future but the unimaginable distant past, we should encounter the same sort of thing" (*Conflict*, p. 39). But Genesis 1 is *sui generis*; it is to be interpreted only on its own merits, and only by means of a serious attempt to ascertain the meaning of the author.

little bearing upon how Genesis one is to be interpreted. Genesis one must be interpreted upon its own merit.

8. Analogy of Other Passages

This same consideration must be emphasized in answer to the appeal made to other passages of Scripture. Thus, it is pointed out that certain visions of John, although they are heptadic in structure, nevertheless, do not exhibit a strictly chronological sequence. Whether they exhibit a chronological sequence or not may sometimes be difficult to determine, but it is really an irrelevant consideration, for even if all the events in Revelation were narrated without regard for chronological considerations, that fact in itself would not prove that the first chapter of Genesis was to be so interpreted. Although the book of Revelation is identified as containing words of prophecy, it nevertheless is an apocalypse in the sense that Daniel also is an apocalypse. Together with the book of Daniel it forms a unique literary genre which is not matched or equalled by the non-canonical apocalypses. It is not always to be interpreted in the same manner as writing which is truly historical. If, therefore, there are passages in Revelation which are to be interpreted in a non-chronological manner, this in itself is really an irrelevant consideration. It has nothing to do with the manner in which the historical writing of Genesis one is to be interpreted. If Revelation is to be a guide for the interpretation of Genesis one, then it must be shown that Genesis one is of the same literary genre as Revelation. This, we believe, cannot be successfully done.

In this connection it may be remarked that appeal to other passages of Scripture in which a non-chronological order of statement is found is really beside the point. No one denies that there are such passages. What must be denied is the idea that the presence of such passages somehow supports the view that Genesis one is to be interpreted non-chronologically.[71]

(to be concluded)

[71] The following passages are generally adduced in this connection, Gen. 2; II Kg. 23:4–10; Ps. 78:44 ff.; Matt. 4:1–11; Lk. 4:13, 16–30; Matt. 13:53–58. *Cf. Conflict*, pp. 37 f.

IV. *The Fourth Commandment and the Scheme
Six Plus One*

The fourth commandment actually refutes the non-chronological interpretation of Genesis one. It is to the credit of Professor Ridderbos that he recognizes the difficulty and endeavors to provide an explanation.[72] He candidly states that we do not know what led the Israelite to work six days and to rest a seventh, other than the influence of God's providence. Hence, the author of Genesis one could present his material in such a way as to give the impression that God worked six days and rested one day.

The "rest" of God, argues Ridderbos correctly, is to be regarded as creation's climax, and this rest was expressed by mentioning the seventh day. Man, according to the fourth commandment, is to work as God worked. He is not, however, to be a slave to his work, but, as God rested, so man at the proper time is to lay aside his work for rest. His work, like that of God, is to have the glory of God as its goal. The numbers of Genesis one, therefore, it is reasoned, have symbolic values.[73]

[72] *Quarterly*, p. 227.

[73] *Conflict*, p. 41. H. J. Nieboer (*Lucerna*, p. 645), in speaking of the problem, remarks, "het ligt echter voor de hand aan te nemen, dat voor ons als westerse mensen — met lineaal, weegschaal en chronometer — zich hier een probleem voordoet, dat voor de gelovige Israëliet, wiens cultus vol was van symbolische transposities, helemaal niet bestond". A position that requires this type of defense must be weak indeed. Ezekiel had a measuring rod (Ezekiel 40:3); Amos knew what a plumbline was (Amos 7:7); the ark was constructed according to certain measurements, so also were the tabernacle and temple. And as for the matter of weights we may note Deuteronomy 25:13–16. Nor should we forget Ahaz' sundial (Isaiah 38:8).

It should be noted that the seventh day is to be interpreted as similar

In accordance with his decree — for Ridderbos rightly desires to retain the idea that the Sabbath ordinance is rooted in creation — God designated the seventh day as a day of rest, and so the number seven became a sacred number, "the number of the completed cycle", and this pattern is presupposed in the ten commandments.

There are, however, serious difficulties in any attempt to square a non-chronological scheme of the days of Genesis with the fourth commandment. One must agree, whatever position he is defending, that, irrespective of their length, the periods mentioned in Genesis one may legitimately be designated by the Hebrew word יוֹם (day). The fundamental question is whether or not Genesis one presents a succession of six days followed by a seventh. According to Exodus 20 such is the case. "Six days shalt thou labor and do all thy work", is the divine command, and the reason given for obedience thereto is rooted in God's creative work, "for in six days the Lord made heaven and earth". Man, therefore, according to the Ten Commandments, is to work for six consecutive days, inasmuch as God worked for six consecutive days.

The whole structure of the week is rooted and grounded in the fact that God worked for six consecutive days and rested a seventh. For this reason we are commanded to remember (זָכוֹר) the Sabbath day. Man is to "remember" the Sabbath day, for God has instituted it. There would be no point in the command, "Remember the Sabbath day", if God had not instituted the day. The human week derives validity and significance from the creative week. Indeed, the very Hebrew word for week (שָׁבוּעַ) means "that which is divided into seven", "a besevened thing".[74] The fourth commandment

---

in nature to the preceding six days. There is no Scriptural warrant whatever (certainly not Hebrews 4:3–5) for the idea that this seventh day is eternal. Visée (*op. cit.*, p. 640) is on good ground when he writes "En al evenmin laat zich als tegenargument (*i. e.*, against the position that the days were solar days) aanvoeren, dat de zevende dag, nog zou voortduren. De Zevende dag van Genesis 2:2 en 3 is kennelijk een dag in de bekende zin geweest, de dag, die God de HEERE als de dag, waarop Hij zelf gerust heeft (perfectum), voor zijn schepsel gezegend heeft."

[74] שָׁבוּעַ — lit., a heptad. The form appears to be a Qal passive participle, at least in passages such as Gen. 29:27, 28; Lev. 12:5; Jer. 5:24. On the

constitutes a decisive argument against any non-chronological scheme of the six days of Genesis one. And a non-chronological scheme destroys the reason for observance of a six-day week followed by a seventh day of rest.

The scheme of six days followed by a seventh is also deeply embedded in the literature of the ancient near east.

In Tablet XI of the Gilgamesh Epic, for example, we read (lines 127–130),

> Six days and six (nights)
> Did the wind blow, the rain, the tempest and the flood overwhelmed the land.
> When the seventh day came, the tempest, the flood
> Which had battled like an army, subsided in its on-slaught.[75]

The reference is to the six days of the downpour of the flood, days which are followed by a seventh. The meaning of course is that for a space of six days the winds blew and the rain fell. Certainly there would be no warrant for interpreting the phrase "six days" otherwise. Yet, inasmuch as it is used in precisely the same manner, if in the Gilgamesh epic the phrase "six days" means six consecutive days, why does it not have the same meaning in Exodus 20?

Again, in Tablet XI (lines 142–146) we read,

> Mount Nisir held fast the ship and did not allow it to move,
> One day, a second day did the Mount Nisir hold the ship firm.
> A third day, a fourth day did the Mount Nisir hold the ship firm.

---

other hand, in certain instances the word is written with a naturally long *a*, *e. g.*, Dan. 9:24; Num. 28:26; Dan. 10:2, 3; Ex. 34:22.

[75] The text is found in R. Campbell Thompson: *The Epic of Gilgamesh*, Oxford, 1930. The comment of Böhl (*Het Gilgamesj-Epos Nationaal Heldendicht van Babylonie*, 1952, Amsterdam, p. 81) is interesting. "Na een week (aanmerkelijk eerder dan volgens het bijbelse verhaal) houdt de vloed op." How else can the words of the text be understood? "Na een week" is the natural understanding that one would receive from the cuneiform text.

When the seventh day came,
I sent forth a dove and dismissed her.[76]

Here the idea of succession is made very clear. The pattern is six successive days followed by a seventh. A similar pattern is given in the description of the loaves which the wife of Utnapishtim bakes for him.

His first loaf of bread was completely dried,
the second - - - the third - - - moist; the fourth white - - -
the fifth moldy; the sixth just baked - - -
the seventh - - - - the man awoke (tablet XI, lines
215–218).[77]

Here six distinct loaves are mentioned, and at the mention of the seventh, after the six have been described, Utnapishtim touches the man, and he awakes. It is difficult to avoid the conclusion that in the order of the description of the loaves chronology is present.

In the Babylonian Creation Account (Enuma Elish) we read in the fifth tablet (lines 16, 17),

Thou shalt shine with horns to make known six days;
On the seventh day with (hal)f a tiara [78]

Here the shining forth is to occupy the space of six days, and the seventh day which follows is climactic.

The same scheme of six days followed by a seventh is also found in the literature of Ugarit.[79] The following examples will suffice:

Go a day, and a second, a third, a fourth day,
a fifth, a sixth day, with the sun,
On the seventh day, then thou shalt arrive at Udm.
(*Keret* I iii, lines 2–4).

[76] Note the emphasis that is placed on the seventh day. "VII-a ûma (ma) i-na ka-ša-a-di" (tablet XI, line 145). The same phrase *i-na ka-ša-a-di* is also used in line 129.

[77] Here again the seventh day is climactic.

[78] The text is given in L. King: *The Seven Tablets of Creation*, 2 vols., 1902. *Cf.* also A. Heidel: *The Babylonian Genesis*, Chicago, 1951, which gives an excellent translation and commentary.

[79] The texts will be found in Cyrus H. Gordon: *Ugaritic Handbook*, Rome, 1955, and in G. R. Driver: *Canaanite Myths and Legends*, Edinburgh, 1956.

- - - - - - remain quiet a day, and a second,
a third, a fourth day, a fifth,
a sixth day, thine arrow do not send
to the town, the stones of thy hand
in succession cast. And behold, the sun
On the seventh day, etc.

(Keret I iii, lines 10–15).

Behold! a day and a second he fed
the Kathirat, and gave drink to the shining daughters
of the moon; a third, a fourth day, - - -
- - - - - - - - a fifth
a sixth day - - - - - - - - -
Behold! on the seventh day - - - -.

(Aqhat II ii, lines 32–39).

Behold! - - - - - day, and a second, did devour
the fire - - - in the houses, the flames
in the palace, a third, a fourth day,
did the fire devour in the houses
a fifth, a sixth day did devour
fire in the houses, flames
in the midst of the palaces. Behold!
on the seventh day there was extinguished the fire.

(Baal II vi, lines 24–32).

From the evidence just adduced it is clear that in the ancient near eastern world there was recognized a scheme of six successive days or items followed by a climactic seventh. In its best known form this scheme appears in the ordinary week. That man thus began to distinguish the days did not derive from chance. It was rooted in the very creation. Men are to remember the Sabbath day for that was the day on which God rested from his labors. In adopting a six-day week climaxed by a seventh day of rest, mankind was obedient to its Creator, who also had worked for six days and rested on the seventh.

V. *The Nature and Structure of Genesis One*

Genesis one is a document *sui generis*; its like or equal is not to be found anywhere in the literature of antiquity.[80] And the reason for this is obvious. Genesis one is a divine revelation to man concerning the creation of heaven and earth. It does not contain the cosmology of the Hebrews or of Moses. Whatever that cosmology may have been, we do not know. Had they not been the recipients of special revelation their cosmology probably would have been somewhat similar to that of the Babylonians. There is no reason to believe that their ideas as to the origin of the heavens and earth would have been more "advanced" than those of their neighbors. Israel, however, was favored of God in that he gave to her a revelation concerning the creation of heaven and earth,[81] and Genesis one is that revelation.

Genesis one is written in exalted, semi-poetical language; nevertheless, it is not poetry. For one thing the characteristics

[80] For this reason we cannot properly speak of the literary genre of Genesis one. It is not a cosmogony, as though it were simply one among many. In the nature of the case a true cosmogony must be a divine revelation. The so-called "cosmogonies" of the various peoples of antiquity are in reality deformations of the originally revealed truth of creation. There is only one genuine cosmogony, namely, Genesis one, and this account alone gives reliable information as to the origin of the earth. Nor is Genesis one an epic of creation, for an epic is actually a narrative poem that centers about the exploits of some hero. Whether in writing Genesis one Moses by divine inspiration was led to express the truth in a literary form, which by its use of recurring phrases and small compact units, was similar to literary forms of Canaan is difficult to determine. Gray, for example (*The Legacy of Canaan*, Leiden, 1957, p. 213), remarks that there are no exact replicas of the Canaanite literary types in the Old Testament although he does think that some of the main features and much of the imagery familiar in the Canaanite myth are found in the myth of the conflict of Cosmos and Chaos which, according to Gray, was adopted by the Hebrews. With this latter thought we cannot agree, for we do not believe that there is evidence extant to support the view that the Hebrews ever adopted any myth of the conflict of Cosmos and Chaos. The basic reason why Moses used the device of six days was that creation occurred in six days.

[81] This conclusion follows inasmuch as Genesis one is a part of the holy Scriptures. In *Thy Word Is Truth* (Grand Rapids, 1957) I have set forth the reasons why I believe the Bible to be the Word of God.

of Hebrew poetry are lacking, and in particular there is an absence of parallelism. It is true that there is a division into paragraphs, but to label these strophes does not render the account poetic. The Bible does contain poetic statements of creation, namely, Job 38:8–11 and Psalm 104:5–9. Ridderbos aptly points out that if one will read Genesis 1:6–8; Job 38:8–11 and Psalm 104:5–9 in succession he will feel the difference between the Genesis account and the poetic accounts.[82] The latter two passages are poetic for they contain parallelism, and it is this feature which is lacking in the first chapter of the Bible.

Genesis one is the prelude to a severely historical book, a book so strongly historical that it may be labeled genealogical. Indeed, the first chapter stands in an intimate relationship with what follows. By its usage of the phrase הַשָּׁמַיִם וְהָאָרֶץ Genesis 2:4a connects the prelude (Gen. 1:1–2:3) with the genealogical section of the book. It is an intimate relationship, for chapters two and three clearly presuppose the contents of chapter one. This is seen among other things in the usage of the phrase יְהוָה אֱלֹהִים which is intended to identify יְהוָה with the אֱלֹהִים of chapter one.[83] Furthermore, chapter two assumes the creation of the earth, the heaven and the sea, the account of which is given in chapter one.

The chapter is thus seen to constitute an integral part of the entire book and is to be regarded as sober history. By this we mean that it recounts what actually transpired. It is reliable and trustworthy, for it is the special revelation of God. If this involves conflicts with what scientists assert, we cannot escape difficulties by denying the historical character of

[82] *Conflict*, p. 36. The following quotation from Visée (*op. cit.*, p. 636) makes an interesting point. "In Genesis 2 komt wel een dichterlijk gedeelte voor. Reeds B. Wielenga heeft er op gewezen dat we in Adams bruidegomslied te doen hebben met het eerste lied. Maar juist dit om z'n poëtische vorm in deze prozaïsche omgeving terstond opvallende lied accentueert destemeer het niet-poëtisch karakter der eerste hoofdstukken." The reference is to Wielenga's book, *De Bijbel als boek van schoonheid*, Kampen, 1925, pp. 237, 238, a work which I have not seen.

[83] For examples of double names of deity in the ancient near east see the informative article of K. A. Kitchen: "Egypt and the Bible: Some Recent Advances", in *Faith and Thought*, Vol. 91, Nos. 2 and 3 (Winter 1959, Summer 1960), pp. 189, 190.

Genesis. We cannot agree, for example, with Vawter, when he writes, "It is therefore apparent that we should not be seeking a concord between the poetry of Genesis and the scientifically established data on the development of the universe".[84] To dismiss Genesis one as poetry, and it is Genesis one of which Vawter is speaking, is to refuse to face the facts.

At the same time, although Genesis one is an historical account, it is clear, as has often been pointed out, that Moses does employ a certain framework for the presentation of his material. This may be described by the terms fiat and fulfillment,[85] and the scheme may be represented as follows:

1. The divine speech   "And God said"
2. The fiat   "Let there be"
3. The fulfillment   "And there was" or
                      "and it was so"
4. The judgment   "And God saw that it was good"
5. Conclusion   "And there was evening
                      and there was morning"

A careful study of Genesis one, however, will show that this arrangement is not consistently carried through for each of the days. Indeed, even the mere fiat-fulfillment is not con-

---

[84] *A Pathway Through Genesis*, New York, 1956, p. 48. Nor is it consistent to regard the entire chapter as a figurative scheme and yet hold that it teaches that God is the creator of all. For if we interpret the greater part of the chapter as not corresponding to what actually happened (and how can the non-chronological view escape this?) by what warrant may we say that Genesis 1:1 corresponds to what did happen? We have not then derived the doctrine of creation from this chapter by exegesis, but have simply assumed it in an a priori fashion. For the so-called "framework" hypothesis demands inconsistency of its adherents. It tells them that they themselves may choose what in Genesis one corresponds to reality. Surely such an hypothesis cannot be regarded as exegetically well grounded. Visée (*op. cit.*, p. 639) is to the point when he writes, "En niets geeft ons het recht allerlei zakelijke en feitelijke gegevens uit Genesis 1 te elimineren en het geheel te verschralen tot de hoofdsom, 'dat alles van God is.' "

[85] Oswald T. Allis: "Old Testament Emphases and Modern Thought", in *Princeton Theological Review*, Vol. XXIII (July 1925), p. 443. Kramer points out (*op. cit.*, p. 9) that the fiats of Genesis one have a parallel in the words of Enki, "Let him bring up the water, etc.". He also calls attention to the repetitions in lines 42–52 (*cf.* Gen. 1:11) and lines 53–64 (Gen. 1:12) and to the phrase "and it was indeed so" (hur he-na-nam-ma) as a correspondence to וַיְהִי־כֵן.

sistently maintained. Nor can we agree with Deimel that the writer has consistently employed seven different literary elements (the sacred number).[86] These are said to be (1) God said; (2) the fiat; (3) the fulfillment; (4) description of the particular act of creation; (5) God's naming or blessing; (6) the divine satisfaction and (7) the conclusion. These seven literary elements are thought to interlock in the following fashion.

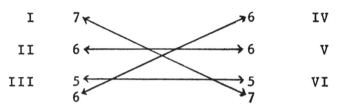

But is this arrangement actually found in Genesis? In the opinion of the writer of this article these literary elements are more accurately enumerated as follows:

I 7   II 8   III 7, 6   IV 9   V 7   VI 5, 10

Thus, on the second day there is actually a double fiat, "let there be an expanse . . . and let it be dividing". In response to this there is also a double fulfillment, "and God made . . . and he divided". On the fifth day, to which the literary elements of the second day are supposed to correspond we find also a double fiat, "let the waters swarm . . . let the birds fly". Corresponding to this, however, although three objects of his creative activity are mentioned, there is but one fulfillment, "and God created". Here, therefore, there is no perfect correspondence of form with the description of the second day.

Again, it is very questionable whether a true correspondence of form can be shown to exist between the third and the sixth days. With respect to the first work of the third day there are actually seven elements, for there is a double fiat, "let

[86] Anton Deimel: *Enuma Eliš und Hexaëmeron*, Rom, 1934, p. 80. "In dem obigen Schema entsprechen sich das 1. und 8. Werk in bezug auf die Zahl der Formeln, 2. und 5. in bezug auf *Zahl* und *Reihenfolge* der Formeln, 2. und 6., 3. und 7. in bezug auf die Zahl der Formeln" (p. 81).

the waters be gathered ... and let the dry land be seen". At this point, however, no fulfillment of these fiats is mentioned, but merely the statement, "and it was so". With respect to the first work of the sixth day, however, there are but five literary elements. There is but one fiat, "let the earth send forth", and this is followed by the statement, "and it was so". Then comes the actual fulfillment in the words, "And God made, etc.". This is quite different from the arrangement of the first work of the third day.

As to the second work of the third day there are six elements; one fiat ("let the earth send forth grass" etc.) followed by the words, "and it was so", and then the fulfillment, "And the earth sent forth grass" etc. Very different in arrangement, however, is the second work of the sixth day. True enough, there are here six elements, but they include a double fiat, followed by the fulfillment, "and God created", and a command of God. This is entirely different in arrangement from the second work of the third day. Furthermore, there is added to the second work of the sixth day an additional "and God said", and this is followed by an "and it was so", and the summary statement, "and God saw everything that he had made" etc., and then the conclusion in which the evening and morning are mentioned.

From this brief analysis, it is evident that we cannot find the exact correspondences which Deimel believes exist in the first chapter of Genesis. It is perhaps accurate to say that the account of creation is told in terms of fiat and fulfillment, although not even this arrangement is carried through consistently. Hence, it would seem that the primary interest of the writer was not a schematic classification or arrangement of material. His primary concern was to relate how God created the heaven and the earth. There is enough in the way of repetitive statement and schematic arrangement to arrest the attention, and when it has arrested the attention, it has fulfilled its function. The arrangement of the material serves the purpose merely of impressing upon the reader's mind the significance of the content.

VI. *Survey of Genesis One: The First Day*

What follows is merely a sketch of the contents of Genesis one, which seeks to point out the progress and development that characterize the chapter. It in no sense pretends to be a full scale commentary. The presence of this chronological succession of events constitutes one of the strongest arguments against any non-chronological view of the days.

Although the beginning of the first day is not mentioned in Genesis one, it would seem from Exodus 20:11 that it began with the absolute creation, the very beginning. After the statement of creation in verse one, the first divine act mentioned is the command, "let there be light". The conditions existing at the time when this command was uttered were those set forth in the second verse of the chapter. Against the dark background described in verse two the light shone forth. As a result of God's speaking, the light sprang into existence. This light is not an emanation from God, nor is it an attribute, but is the result of God's creative Word.

It must be noted that Genesis one teaches the creation of light before the sun, nor is this to be regarded as an accident. Even if the chapter be considered a mere human composition, we may be sure that its author knew well enough that the light of the present-day world comes from the sun. This representation was intentional. And it is well to note that Enuma Elish has the same order. Here also light comes before the sun. Not until the fifth tablet do we meet with a statement of the making of the heavenly bodies. In this respect therefore, namely, relating the production of the heavenly bodies after the existence of light, the Enuma Elish is in agreement with Genesis. When Apsu wishes to revolt, light is already present, for he says: "Their way has become grievous to me. By day I cannot rest, by night I cannot sleep" (1:37, 38). Heidel also points out that there was a radiance or dazzling aureole about Apsu (1:68), "He carried off his splendor and put it on himself".[87] And Marduk him-

---

[87] *Cf.* Heidel; *op. cit.*, p. 101. The light, according to Genesis, does not spring from water, nor is it the result of divine action upon the inert mass of *tehom* (Albright: "Contributions to Biblical Archaeology And Philology", *Journal of Biblical Literature*, Vol. 43, p. 368). According to Genesis, light is the result of the creative Word a.one. Nor can we say that in

self was a solar deity, "Son of the sun-god, the sun god of the gods" (1:102). In Enuma Elish light is really an attribute of the gods; in Genesis it is the creation of God. That such an order should be present in Enuma Elish is what might be expected, for this document represents the garbled version of the truth that finally trickled down to the Babylonians.

Is Genesis, however, correct in its teaching that light was created before the sun? Leupold well remarks, "But it ill behooves man to speak an apodictic word at this point and to claim that light apart from the sun is unthinkable. Why should it be? If scientists now often regard light as merely enveloping the sun but not as an intrinsic part of it, why could it not have existed by itself without being localized in any heavenly body?"[88] In an area so filled with mystery and about which we know so little, who can dare to assert that Moses is in error in declaring that light was created before the sun? Can one prove that the presence of light demands a light-bearer? What about the lightning flash? May there not have been rays of original light? We do not know; what can be said with assurance is that at this point Genesis makes no statement that scientists can disprove.

Perhaps one reason why Genesis mentions light before the sun is to disabuse our minds of the idea that light is dependent upon the sun and to cause us to turn our eyes to God as its creator. "Therefore the Lord", says Calvin, "by the very order of the creation, bears witness that he holds in his hand the light, which he is able to impart to us without the sun and moon".[89] There is also a second reason for this order of statement. The light is necessary for all that follows, and Moses places emphasis upon the light, mentioning it as the specific object of God's approval. Elsewhere we have only

---

throwing off the mythical point of view and adopting a cosmogony in which water was the primal element, Thales, founder of the Ionian school of philosophy, showed that he was influenced by a common milieu which also had influenced the writer of Genesis one.

[88] H. C. Leupold: *Exposition of Genesis*, Columbus, 1942, p. 52. *Cf.* also the interesting remark of U. Cassuto (*A Commentary on the Book of Genesis*, Part I, Jerusalem, 1953, p. 14), במציאות האור הם לפני יצירת המאורות אין כמובן שום קושי, שהרי כל בן אדם יודע שיש אור גם בלי מאורות: אור הברקים למשל.

[89] John Calvin: *Commentaries on The First Book of Moses Called Genesis*, translated by John King, Edinburgh, M.DCCC.XLVII, Vol. I, p. 76.

the general phrase without a specific object, "and God saw that it was good". Only in verse thirty-one is an object again introduced after the verb "saw." Thus:

verse 4   וַיַּרְא אֱלֹהִים אֶת־הָאוֹר כִּי טוֹב

verse 31   וַיַּרְא אֱלֹהִים אֶת־כָּל־אֲשֶׁר עָשָׂה וְהִנֵּה טוֹב מְאֹד

A contrast is thus shown to be present. The first work is pronounced good, and the completed creation likewise. Nor is it accidental that the light is seen to be good. The light is the necessary condition for the existence of all the works that follow in so far as these have respect to the earth. For life on earth light is necessary, and hence the creation of light is first mentioned.[90]

The division between light and darkness as well as their naming is the work of God. When the light was removed by the appearance of darkness, it was evening, and the coming of light brought morning, the completion of a day. The days therefore, are to be reckoned from morning to morning,[91] and the commencement of the first day, we believe, was at the very beginning.[92]

[90] "Endlich ist אוֹר, besonders vor der Trennung von חשֶׁךְ die allgemeinste, den Umfang des gesamten Chaos erfüllende Schöpfung, die darum geziemend am Anfang des Schöpfungswerks steht" (Procksch; *op. cit.*, p. 427). "das Licht ist Grundbedingg. aller Ordng. u. alles Lebens" (Strack: *op. cit.*, p. 1). "ohne Licht kein Leben und keine Ordnung" (Gunkel: *op. cit.*, p. 103).

[91] "Mit der Reihenfolge Abend-Morgen wird ganz klar gesagt, dass der Tag mit dem Morgen beginnt" (Rabast: *op. cit.*, p. 48). When, however, Rabast goes on to say, "Es heisst ja nicht, es war Abend, sondern es wurde Abend. Der Abend ist also der Abschluss des Tages" (*op. cit.*, p. 48), he apparently limits day to the period of light in distinction from the darkness. But the six days of creation are not thus limited by the text. Procksch is quite dogmatic (*op. cit.*, p. 427), "Die Anschauung des ersten Tages ist also vom irdischen, 24 stundigen Tag eines Äquinoktiums hergenommen, wegen v. 11–13 wohl des Frühlingsäquinoktiums, am Morgen beginnend, am Morgen schliessend".

[92] *Cf.* Keil (*op. cit.*, p. 51), "The first evening was not the gloom, which possibly preceded the full burst of light as it came forth from the primary darkness, and intervened between the darkness and full, broad daylight. It was not till after the light had been created, and the separation of the light from the darkness had taken place, that evening came, and after the evening the morning; and this coming of evening (lit., the obscure) and morning (the breaking) formed one, or the first, day. It follows from this

The Second Day

In the work of day one the emphasis falls upon the light, but in day two the earth is the center of attention.[93] Indeed, the purpose of the second day's work is to separate the earth from all that is beyond it. This is done by means of the firmament which divides the waters above it, *i. e.*, beyond it, from those which are beneath it, *i. e.*, those which adhere to the earth.[94]

The order of Genesis, namely, the creation of the firmament after the light, is also paralleled in Enuma Elish. When Ti'amat is slain, Marduk split her open, and half of her he used to form the sky or firmament. Then he fixed the crossbar and posted guards that the waters in that part of her body which was used to form the sky should not escape. Crass as is this mythology it nevertheless reflects, albeit in a greatly mutilated form, the originally revealed truth that the firmament was made after the light and before the appearance of dry land.[95]

From this point on, the chapter concerns itself with the

that the days of creation are not reckoned from evening to evening, but from morning to morning."

[93] "Eigentlich beginnt die Erschaffung der Welt erst mit der Feste (Vers 6); die Erschaffung des Lichts ist vielmehr Vorbedingung des Erschaffens der Welt" (Claus Westermann: *Der Schöpfungsbericht vom Anfang der Bibel*, Stuttgart, 1960, p. 17). This emphasis seems to be more accurate than that of Gunkel (*op. cit.*, p. 104) who labels the work of the second day "Schöpfung des Himmels".

[94] רָקִיעַ, *i. e.*, that which is hammered, beaten out. *Cf.* Isa. 42:5; Ps. 136:6 and the Phoenician מרקע "plating" (Cooke: *North Semitic Inscriptions*, Oxford, 1903, p. 75). Note also the LXX στερέωμα and Vulgate *firmamentum*, which are satisfactory renderings. I am unable to accept the opinion that the waters above the expanse refer to the clouds, for this position does not do justice to the language of the text which states that these waters are *above* the expanse.

[95] The account of the making of the "firmament" is found on Tablet IV, lines 137–139, which may be rendered,

> He split her open like an oyster? (nu-nu mas-di-e)
> into two parts,
> Half of her he set up, and the sky (ša-ma-ma)
> he made as a covering,
> He made fast the par-ku (crossbar? bolt?)
> and watchmen he stationed.

waters under the expanse. In the nature of the case the creation of the firmament must have preceded the division between land and earthbound waters; it could not possibly have followed it. The work of day two, therefore, has to be chronologically previous to that of day three.

The Third Day

Light has been created in order that the dry land may be adorned with verdure, and the firmament has been made that the waters underneath it may be gathered into one place. A twofold fiat introduces the work. First, the water under heaven is to be gathered into one place, and secondly, the dry land is to appear, and the fulfillment is simply stated by the words "and it was so". The magnitude of the work to be accomplished baffles the imagination and yet, in the simple words, "and it was so", the accomplishment is recorded. Nothing is said about means or method of accomplishment that we may concentrate in wonder and adoration upon him who alone can perform such a marvel. "Me will ye not fear, saith the LORD, or from before me will ye not writhe, I who have placed the sand as a boundary to the sea, an eternal statute, nor will it pass over it" (Jer. 5:22a).

If process is here involved, Scripture does not mention that fact; the entire stress appears to be upon the directness with which the task was accomplished. At the same time, it could well be that in this work of division there were tremendous upheavals, so that the mountains were formed and the processes of erosion set in motion.

The land is named, and from this point on the word indicates the dry land in distinction from the ocean. Likewise, the collection of the waters God called "seas", the word being plural in order to indicate the extensive and vast surface covered by water.

All has been preparatory for the second work of the third day, the covering of the land with foliage. With his word God empowers the earth to bring forth plants, and with this fact a certain progress in the order of statement may be noted. Up to this point all had been produced by God's creative word, and all that was produced was inorganic; light, firmament, gathering of waters, dry land. With God's command to the earth, however, there comes into existence objects that are organic, and yet do not move about.

The language of verse eleven is closely guarded, for it precludes the idea that life can originate apart from God or that the earth of itself can produce life. The earth upon which man is to live is one that is hospitable to him, providing him with seed-bearing plants and fruit-bearing trees, but it is only the creative command of God which makes this possible. In vegetation there is distinction, as in the entire creation, so that all man's needs will be met. This distinction together with the idea of propagation according to its kind,[96] supports the idea of order in the entire creation and yet at the same time emphasizes the individuality of each plant.[97]

Lastly, it must be stressed that the plants and trees did

---

[96] The word מִין in verse eleven, whatever its etymology, is a general term and is not the equivalent of our "species", as this word is technically employed. It does not rule out the production of freaks or the possibility of hybrids. It means merely that the producer will beget what is essentially the same as itself. Hence, this term clearly rules out the possibility of one "kind" reproducing anything that is essentially different from itself.

It is perhaps impossible to state precisely what range is included by the term מִין. For that reason, it is wiser to speak in broad terms. The term would exclude the idea that man could have evolved from lower forms of life, from that which was not man. It would also exclude the idea that animal life came from plant life or that a fish might ever change into something essentially different from itself. Hence, caution must be exercised by those who classify animal and plant life. The following statement, appearing in *Bezinning, loc. cit.*, p. 19, by J. Veldkamp, is untenable as well as incautious, "Evolutie is een vaststaand feit. Niet alleen de evolutie in de soorten (sprekende voorbeelden zijn de ontwikkelingsreeken van zoogdieren, zoals paard, neushoorn en olifant), maar ook tussen de soorten (overgangen van vis naar amfibie, van amfibie naar reptiel, van reptiel naar vogel en zoogdier)". For one thing to describe the *ontwikkelingsreeken* in the kinds, the term evolution is inaccurate. Nothing has developed in a manner that was not essentially according to its kind. Great caution must be exercised in describing the so-called changes within kinds. The last part of Veldkamp's statement cannot be defended.

[97] "Es handelt sich hier lediglich um eine Einteilung der Pflanzen, die schon die praktische Verwertbarkeit für Mensch und Tier anzeigt; und diese praktische Einteilung hat zu jeder Zeit ihre Bedeutung" (Rabast, *op. cit.*, p. 51). It should be noted also that the difference among the "kinds" of plants was original; they did not all "descend" from a common ancestor.

not have nor did they need the light of the sun. That this is a scientifically accurate description cannot be questioned,[98] but Calvin's beautiful statement probably brings out the basic reason, "in order that we might learn to refer all things to him, he did not then make use of the sun or moon" (*op. cit., in loc.*). That the earth constantly produces for the benefit of man is not to be ascribed to "nature" but goes back to the creative Word of God.[99]

The Fourth Day

If it be raised as an objection to the accuracy of the Genesis narrative that it is geocentric, the answer must be that it is geocentric only in so far as the earth is made the center of the writer's attention.[100] Even though we are dealing with a divine revelation, nevertheless the human author was a holy man who spake from God (II Pet. 1:21), and he wrote from the standpoint of an earth dweller. The most advanced astronomer of our day will speak of the sunrise and the sunset and of sending *up* a rocket. Such language is geocentric, but it is not in error. Genesis one also speaks from the standpoint of the earth dweller, and in that respect may be labeled geocentric, but none of its statements is contrary to fact. It does not claim that the earth is the physical center of the universe.

By means of the work of the third day the earth was prepared to receive its inhabitants. Before they are placed upon the earth, however, the present arrangement of the universe must be constituted. For the regulation of earth's days and

---

[98] "Durch bestimmte Experimente weiss man ferner, dass sogar die Pflanzen nicht vom Sonnenlicht abhängig sein müssen, so sehr sie es auch heute sind" (Rabast, *op. cit.*, p. 69).

[99] There is no evidence to support the contention of von Rad (*op. cit.*, p. 53) that the earth is called to maternal participation in the act of creation, or that ancient thoughts about a "mother earth" are prominent here. Nor is Gunkel (*op. cit.*, p. 104) correct in saying, "Zu Grunde liegt die Naturbeobachtung von der Fruchtbarkeit des Bodens, wenn er im Frühling soeben austrocknet".

[100] "It is not reflection on the Genesis account to say that it is *geo*centric. It *is* geocentric, because the earth is the abode of man and the scene of his redemption, the story of which is told in the Bible" (Allis: *God Spake By Moses*, Philadelphia, 1951, p. 12).

seasons, there must now be light from a specific source which will rule the day and the night. Hence, the sun and moon are made, a truth which is reflected even in Enuma Elish. In the Babylonian document, however, the order is reversed, namely, stars, moon and sun. In the ancient oriental religions, the stars were considered to be divinities, and possibly for that reason appear first in Enuma Elish. In Genesis, however, mention of the stars appears almost as an afterthought. This is intentional, for while it brings the stars into the picture, it does so in such a way that they are not made prominent.[101] Emphasis is placed, not upon the stars, but upon God, their maker.

Marduk, in the epic, entrusts night to the moon, and what is said of the moon calls to mind the more beautiful biblical statement, "the lesser light to rule the night" (Gen. 1:16). The existence of the sun, however, is assumed in the Babylonian document, and there is no express mention of its formation.[102]

[101] Von Rad's comment (*op. cit.*, p. 43) is quite penetrating. "Vielleicht hängt mit dieser Betonung ihrer Kreaturlichkeit die merkwürdige Trennung von Lichtschöpfung und Erschaffung der Gestirne zusammen. Die Gestirne sind in keiner Weise lichtschöpferisch, sondern durchaus nur Zwischenträger eines Lichtes, das auch ohne sie und vor ihnen da war."

[102] "Im babylonischen Schöpfungsbericht ist die Erschaffung der Gestirne das erste Werk Marduks nach dem Drachenkampf." "Aber die Ähnlichkeit des Wortlauts der beiden Sätze (*i. e.*, Gen. 1:16 and Enuma Elish V. 12) macht hier den tiefen Abstand nur noch deutlicher. Der Mondgott Sin ist in Babylon einer der Hauptgötter; er war von überragender Bedeutung in ganz früher und dann wieder in ganz später Zeit; aber von ihm kann gesagt werden; dass er von einem anderen Gott geschaffen und in sein Herrschaftsamt eingesetzt ist!" (Westermann: *op. cit.*, p. 20). We may render Tablet V:1-4 as follows:

> He erected stations for the great gods
> The stars (kakkabāni) their likenesses, the signs of the zodiac (lu-ma-si) he set up
> He fixed the year (šatta), the signs he designed
> For twelve months (arḫe) he set three stars each.

The creation of the moon is related in V:12 ff.:

> The moon (ᵢˡ Nannar-ru) he caused to shine forth, the night he entrusted (to her)
> He set her as an ornament (šu-uk-nat) of the night unto the setting (*i. e.*, the determining) of the days (a-na ud-du-u û-me).

Very different, however, is the narrative of Genesis. Here the sun is first mentioned, for the sun rules the day upon earth, and man, who is to rule the earth, needs the sunlight first and foremost. For the night time the lesser light-bearer is to rule. Of yet less importance for man are the stars, and hence they are mentioned last.

That the heavenly bodies are made on the fourth day and that the earth had received light from a source other than the sun is not a naive conception, but is a plain and sober statement of the truth.[103] It should be noted, however, that the work of the fourth day is not a *creatio ex nihilo*, but simply a making of the heavenly bodies. The material from which the sun, moon and stars were made was created, *i. e.*, brought into existence, at the absolute beginning. On the fourth day God made of this primary material the sun and moon and stars, so that we may correctly assert that the creation of these heavenly bodies was completed on this day. In similar vein we may also say that on the third day the creation of our globe was completed, although the primal material of the globe was first brought into existence at the absolute beginning. If we were to employ the language of day four with respect to the first work of day three we might then say that although the earth (*i. e.*, in its original form) was created in the beginning, nevertheless, on day three God made the earth. Inasmuch as this is so, the formation of the heavenly bodies may be presumed to have proceeded side by

---

Monthly without ceasing with a tiara go forth (u-sir)
At the beginning of the month, (the time of) shining forth over the lands
With horns shalt thou shine for the determining of six days
On the seventh day (i-na ûm 7-kam) with half a crown.

[103] "Nun ist darüber schon genug gespottet worden, dass hier das Licht vor den Himmelskörpern geschaffen wird. Naturwissenschaftlich ist dies heute kein Problem mehr, denn der Begriff ‚Urstrahlung' besagt genau dasselbe." "Auch wird uns hier keine kindlich naive Auffassung vorgeführt, denn zur Zeit der Aufzeichnung der Genesis wusste wohl auch der Dümmste schon, dass das Tageslicht mit der Sonne zusammenhängt" (Rabast: *op. cit.*, pp. 47, 48). And again, "Das Lachen darüber, dass es schon Licht vor der Erschaffung der Sonne gegeben haben muss, gehört einer vergangenen Zeit an, und eine solche Tatsache ist der modernen kosmischen Physik mit ihrer ‚Urstrahlung' kein Problem mehr" (*idem*, p. 69).

side with that of the earth, and on day four their formation as sun, moon and stars was completed. The reason why Genesis says nothing about the step by step development of the heavenly bodies is that its purpose is to concentrate upon the formation of this earth.

The origin of heaven and earth, however, was simultaneous, but the present arrangement of the universe was not constituted until the fourth day. The establishment of this arrangement is expressed by the verb וַיִּתֵּן, but we are not told how God "gave" or "set" these light-bearers in the firmament. What is of importance is to note that the universe is not an accidental arrangement, but was constituted in orderly fashion by God.

Day four and day one do not present two aspects of the same subject. Indeed, the differences between the two days are quite radical. On day one light is created (וַיְהִי); on day four God makes light-bearers. No function is assigned to the light of day one, but several functions to the light-bearers. God himself divides the light which he has created from the darkness;[104] the light-bearers are to divide between the light and the darkness. It is important to note this function. The light and the darkness between which the light-bearers are to make a division *are already present*. They have manifested themselves in the evening and morning which closed each day. How a division was hitherto made between them we are not told; it is merely stated that God divided between them (1:4). From the fourth day on, however, the division between them is to be made by light-bearers.[105] This

---

[104] "The creation of light, however, was no annihilation of darkness, no transformation of the dark material of the world into pure light, but a separation of the light from the primary matter, a separation which established and determined that interchange of light and darkness, which produces the distinction between day and night" (Keil: *op. cit.*, p. 50). "Die Scheidung (*i. e.*, between light and darkness) ist räumlich, indem die Lichtmasse und die Finsternismasse je eine Hälfte des Chaos einnehmen, zugleich aber zeitlich indem Tag und Nacht entsteht" (Procksch: *op. cit.*, p. 427).

[105] מָאוֹר *luminary*. Von Rad (*op. cit.*, p. 42) thinks that the expression is intended to be prosaic and degrading (prosaisch und degradierend), and that these objects purposely are not named "sun" and "moon" in order to remove every tempting connection (in Umgehung jeder Versuchlichkeit). The words Shemesh and Yareach were of course names of divinities.

one consideration in itself is sufficient to refute the idea that days one and four present two aspects of the same subject. The light-bearers are made for the purpose of dividing between already existing light and darkness. Day four, we may assert with all confidence, presupposes the existence of the light which was created in day one and the darkness which was mentioned in verse two.

The Fifth Day

With the fifth day progress in the writer's mode of statement is apparent. There are now to be produced those creatures which are animate and which move about. Moses uses the verb בָּרָא to designate the creation of three varieties of creatures, namely, the great sea monsters, every living thing that moves about and every winged fowl.[106] Upon all of these a blessing is pronounced, and the content of that blessing is given. By means of the work of the first four days the earth is now prepared to receive life.

It goes without saying that day five does not form an adequate parallel to day two. The sea creatures of day five belong, not to the waters of day two but to the seas of the first work of day three. The seas were formed in day three; the primal waters, however, are mentioned as existing in verse two. Furthermore, the realm in which the birds are to rule is not the firmament but the earth, which also was made in day three.

---

[106] "Mit Nachdruck wird der Begriff בָּרָא v. 21 (cf. v. 27) dafür gebraucht wie v. 1, weil das Leben gegenüber der leblosen Schöpfung etwas spezifisch Neues ist, aus ihren Stoffen und Kräften unableitbar" (Procksch: op. cit., p. 430). There is no evidence to support Procksch's statement, "der Begriff ברא entspricht der Theologie von P, der Begriff הוציא einer altertümlichen, von P wohl übernommenen Naturphilosophie, nach der ‚Mutter Erde' alles Lebendige auf ihr gebiert (cf. ψ 139, 15)" (op. cit., p. 431). Aalders is in accord with the total scriptural emphasis when he writes, "Het spreekt vanzelf dat we hier evenmin als bij de plantenwereld te denken hebben aan een vermogen dat in de aarde zelf gelegen was . . . door den Goddelijke wil kwamen de dieren uit de aarde voort" (op. cit., p. 93).

As on the third so on the sixth day two works are mentioned. On the third day the earth had brought forth plants
and on the sixth it is to bring forth the animals. Instead,
however, of a statement that the earth did bring forth the
animals, we are told that God made them (verse 25). It may
be that this manner of statement is deliberately chosen to
refute the concept of a mother earth, for in many of the
cosmogonies of antiquity it is the earth which of herself
produces the animals. Here the emphasis is upon the fact
that God made the animals.

At the same time at this point (verse 25) Moses uses עָשָׂה
and not בָּרָא. With בָּרָא (in verse 21) there had followed an
accompanying blessing (verse 22), and likewise in the second
work of the sixth day a blessing accompanies בָּרָא. Here
there is no blessing, and hence עָשָׂה is used. The blessing of
the sixth day is not appended to each individual work but
only to the second, the creation of man who is to rule over
the animals. Hence, it may not be amiss to claim that in-
directly, at least, the animals are blessed, even though no
express blessing is pronounced over them.

That the creation of man is the crowning work of the
narrative and presupposes what has previously been narrated,
hardly needs to be mentioned. The second work of the sixth
day presupposes the first, and both presuppose the work of
the fifth day. Were this not so, the command to rule over
the fish of the sea and the fowl of the air (verse 28) would be
meaningless.

That man is not merely one of the animals is also emphasized by the fact that God engages in deliberation with himself
concerning the creation of man.[107] Furthermore, man is
created in the image of God, and upon him a divine blessing is
pronounced in which his position as ruler over all things is set
forth. The chapter then closes with a pronouncement as to

---

[107] "Aber ebenso klar ist auch, dass der Mensch grundsätzlich von allen
Tieren verschieden ist. Das wird sogar schon rein formal deutlich gemacht:
Einerseits wechselt noch einmal das Metrum in den Gottessprüchen."
"Anderseits findet sich bei der Erschaffung des Menschen eine besondere
feierliche Einleitung" (Rabast: *op. cit.*, pp. 57, 58).

the nature of all that God had made, namely, that it was very good.

It is this remarkable fact of progression, both in method of statement and in actual content, which proves that the days of Genesis are to be understood as following one another chronologically.[108] When to this there is added the plain chronological indications, day one, day two, etc., climaxing in *the* sixth day (note that the definite article appears only with the sixth day) all support for a non-chronological view is removed.

In this connection the question must be raised, "If a non-chronological view of the days be admitted, what is the purpose of mentioning six days?" For, once we reject the chronological sequence which Genesis gives, we are brought to the point where we can really say very little about the content of Genesis one. It is impossible to hold that there are two trios of days, each paralleling the other. Day four, as has already been pointed out, speaks of God's placing the light-bearers in the firmament. The firmament, however, had been made on the second day. If the fourth and the first days are two aspects of the same thing, then the second day also (which speaks of the firmament) must precede days one and four. If this procedure be allowed, with its wholesale disregard of grammar, why may we not be consistent and equate all four of these days with the first verse of Genesis? There is no defense against such a procedure, if once we abandon the clear language of the text. In all seriousness it must be asked, Can we believe that the first chapter of Genesis intends to teach that day two preceded days one and four? To ask that question is to answer it.[109]

There is, of course, a purpose in the mention of the six days. It is to emphasize the great contrast between the unformed universe of verse two and the completed world of

---

[108] *Cf.* Young: "Genesis One And Natural Science", in *Torch and Trumpet*, Vol. VII, No. 4 (September 1957), pp. 16 f.

[109] It should be noted that if the "framework" hypothesis were applied to the narratives of the virgin birth or the resurrection or Romans 5:12 ff., it could as effectively serve to minimize the importance of the content of those passages as it now does the content of the first chapter of Genesis.

verse thirty-one.[110] Step by step in majestic grandeur God
worked to transform the unformed earth into a world upon
which man might dwell and which man might rule for God's
glory. How noble and beautiful is this purpose, a purpose
which is obscured and even obliterated when once we deny
that the six days are to be taken in sequence. If Moses had
intended to teach a non-chronological view of the days, it is
indeed strange that he went out of his way, as it were, to
emphasize chronology and sequence. We may recall the
thought of Aalders that in the first chapter of Genesis there
is not a hint that the days are to be taken as a mere form or
manner of representation. In other words, if Moses intended
to teach something like the so-called "framework theory" of
the days, why did he not give at least some indication that
such was his intention? This question demands an answer.

VII. The Real Problem in Genesis One

It is questionable whether serious exegesis of Genesis one
would in itself lead anyone to adopt a non-chronological view
of the days for the simple reason that everything in the text
militates against it. Other considerations, it would seem,
really wield a controlling influence. As it stands Genesis
might be thought to conflict with "science". Can Genesis
therefore be taken at face value?[111] This type of approach,
however, as we have been seeking to point out, must be
rejected. One who reads the Gospels will receive the impression
that the body of the Lord Jesus Christ actually emerged from
the tomb and that he rose from the dead. But will not this
first-hand impression cause needless stumbling-blocks in the
path of faith? If we wish to rescue thoughtful people from a
materialistic conception of life will not our purpose be harmed
by an insistence upon miracle? As a recent writer has said,
"The school of opinion that insists upon a physical resurrection will not satisfy a scientifically penetrating mind".[112]

[110] At least in a formal sense von Rad acknowledges this. "Wir sehen
hier, das theologische Denken von 1. Mos. 1 bewegt sich nicht so zwischen
der Polarität: Nichts-Geschaffenes als vielmehr zwischen der Polarität:
Chaos-Kosmos" (*op. cit.*, p. 39).

[111] *Conflict*, p. 29.

[112] *Cf.* the letter of Robert Ericson in *Christianity Today*, Vol. VI, No. 1,
(Oct. 13, 1961), p. 44.

Dare we reason in this way? If we do, we shall soon abandon
Christianity entirely, for Christianity is a supernatural religion of redemption, one of its chief glories being its miracles.
And this brings us to the heart of the matter. In the study of
Genesis one our chief concern must not be to adopt an interpretation that is necessarily satisfying to the "scientifically
penetrating mind". Nor is our principal purpose to endeavor
to make the chapter harmonize with what "science" teaches.
Our principal task, in so far as we are able, is to get at the
meaning which the writer sought to convey.

Why is it so difficult to do this with the first chapter of the
Bible? The answer, we believe, is that although men pay lip
service to the doctrine of creation, in reality they find it a
very difficult doctrine to accept. It is easy to behold the
wonders of the present universe and to come to the conclusion
that things have always been as they are now. To take but
one example, the light of the stars, we are told, travelling at
the rate of about 186,000 miles per second, in some instances
takes years to reach this earth. Hence, men conclude it would
have been impossible for the days of Genesis to have been
ordinary days of twenty-four hours each.[113]

In other words in employing an argument such as this, we
are measuring creation by what we now know, and whether
we wish or not, are limiting the power of God. Why could not
God in the twinkling of an eye have formed the stars so that
their light could be seen from earth? We cannot limit the
creative power of God by what we today have learned from
his providential working.

Those catechisms and creeds which have made a distinction
between God's work of creation and his work of providence
have exhibited a deep and correct insight into the teaching of
Scripture.[114] Creation and providence are to be distinguished,

[113] Allis goes to the heart of the matter when he says "We need to remember, however, that limitless time is a poor substitute for that Omni-
potence which can dispense with time. The reason the account of creation
given here is so simple and so impressive is that it speaks in terms of the
creative acts of an omnipotent God, and not in terms of *limitless* space
and *infinite* time and *endless* process" (*God Spake By Moses*, p. 11). *Cf.*
also Allis' excellent article, "The Time Element in Genesis 1 and 2" in
Torch and Trumpet, Vol. VIII, No. 3 (July-August, 1958), pp. 16–19.
[114] Thus, the Westminster Confession of Faith devotes a chapter to the

and it is not our prerogative, in the name of science, to place limits upon God's creative power. In a helpful article on "The Old Testament and Archaeology", William F. Albright wisely comments respecting the first chapter of Genesis, "In fact, modern scientific cosmogonies show such a disconcerting tendency to be short lived that it may be seriously doubted whether science has yet caught up with the Biblical story".[115]

If the church fathers had insisted that Genesis one conform to the "science" of their day, how tragic the result would have been. Had Luther done the same thing, the result would have been no better. And we must be cautious not to reject Scripture merely because at some points it may appear not to harmonize with what some modern scientists teach. Of one thing we may be sure; the statements of Genesis and the facts of nature are in perfect harmony.

The Bible does not state how old the earth is, and the question of the age of the earth is not the heart of the issue.[116] What is the heart of the issue is whether God truly created or whether we, merely upon the basis of our observations of the universe, can place limits upon the manner in which God worked.

Although the Bible does not state the age of the earth, it does clearly teach that the world was created by the Word of God. The fiat was followed by the repetitive fulfillment. God spake, and his Word accomplished his will. It was a

---

work of creation (chapter IV) and one to that of providence (chapter V). The same distinction appears in the Larger and Shorter Catechisms. Questions 15–17 of the Larger Catechism deal with creation and questions 18–20 with providence. The Shorter Catechism devotes two questions (9, 10) to the work of creation and two (11, 12) to that of providence.

[115] ed. Alleman and Flack: *Old Testament Commentary*, Philadelphia, 1948, p. 135.

[116] "Scientists, who speak in terms of light years, and add cipher to cipher in estimating the time of the beginning of things, ridicule the idea of twenty-four-hour days. But when they multiply thousands to millions and millions to billions and billions to trillions, figures practically cease to have any meaning, and they expose their own ignorance. From the standpoint of those who believe in a God who is omnipotent, and who recognize that time and space are finite and created 'things', this adding on of ciphers is absurd. It is a distinct feature of the miracles of the Bible that they are limited neither by time nor space" (Allis: *God Spake By Moses*, pp. 10 f.).

powerful word that brought his desires to pass. "For he spake,
and it was *done*; he commanded, and it stood fast" (Ps. 33:9);
"by the word of God the heavens were of old" (II Pet. 3:5);
"Through faith we understand that the worlds were framed
by the word of God" (Heb. 11:3).[117]
Before the majestic declarations of Scripture we can but
bow in humble reverence. How meager is our knowledge;
how great our ignorance! Dare we therefore assert that only
in such and such a manner the Creator could have worked?
Are we really in possession of such knowledge that we can
thus circumscribe him? Of course there is much in the first
chapter of Genesis that we cannot understand. There is,
however, one thing that, by the grace of the Creator, we
may do. We may earnestly seek to think the thoughts of
God after him as they are revealed in the mighty first chapter
of the Bible. We can cease being rationalists and become
believers. In the face of all the strident claims to the contrary
we can believe, and we need never be ashamed to believe that
"in six days the Lord made heaven and earth, the sea and all
that in them is" (Ex. 20:11a).

VIII. *Conclusion*

From the preceding examination of Genesis one there are
certain conclusions which may be drawn.

1. The pattern laid down in Genesis 1:1–2:3 is that of six
days followed by a seventh.

2. The six days are to be understood in a chronological
sense, that is, one day following another in succession. This
fact is emphasized in that the days are designated, one, two,
three, etc.[118]

---

[117] It must be noted, however, that process is not necessarily ruled out
by the fiats. In the second work of the third day, for example, there
could very well have been process. We cannot state to what extent process
may have been present. *Cf*. Allis in *Torch and Trumpet*, vol. VIII, No. 3,
p. 18.

[118] There is no exegetical warrant to support the position (*Lucerna*,
p. 645) expressed by H. Nieboer; "Gods scheppingsdagen (werkdagen of
ook dagwerken) zijn steeds present en actueel (aldus dr. J. H. Diemer).
De dagen-van-God zijn aspecten van zijn werkzaamheid, voorheen en

3. The length of the days is not stated. What is important is that each of the days is a period of time which may legitimately be denominated יוֹם ("day").

4. The first three days were not solar days such as we now have, inasmuch as the sun, moon and stars had not yet been made.

5. The beginning of the first day is not indicated, although, from Exodus 20:11, we may warrantably assume that it began at the absolute beginning, Genesis 1:1.

6. The Hebrew word יוֹם is used in two different senses in Genesis 1:5. In the one instance it denotes the light in distinction from the darkness; in the other it includes both evening and morning. In Genesis 2:4b the word is employed in yet another sense, "in the day of the LORD God's making".

7. If the word "day" is employed figuratively, i. e., to denote a period of time longer than twenty-four hours, so also may the terms "evening" and "morning", inasmuch as they are component elements of the day, be employed figuratively.[119] It goes without saying that an historical narrative may contain figurative elements. Their presence, however, can only be determined by means of exegesis.

8. Although the account of creation is told in terms of fiat and fulfillment, this does not necessarily exclude all process. In the second work of the third day, for example,

---

thans. Deze dagen zijn niet met menselijke tijdsmaatstaf te meten, evenmin als bijvoorbeeld het ‚duizendjarig rijk.' Wie dus vraagt naar de tijdsduur van bijvoorbeeld de scheppingsdagen voor de vierde dag en daarna, maakt vanuit dit standpunt gezien dezelfde fout als degene die na een uiteenzetting, in de eerste plaats dit, in de tweede plaats dat, vraagt naar de geografische bepaling en de afmetingen van die plaatsen; of na een betoog in verschillende stappen, naar de lengte in centimeters van die stappen."

[119] "Man hat dafür auf des ויהי ערב ויהי בקר berufen (vgl. ערב בקר Dan. 8, 14 Abend = Morgen = Tag), aber verlieren denn diese Tage die Wahrheit ihres Wesens, wenn der Wechsel von Licht und Dunkel, nach welchem sich ihr Anfang und Ende bestimmt, nach anderen als irdischen zeitlangen gemessen ist und nach andern Gesetzen, als den nun innerhalb unseres Sonnensystems naturgemässen, erfolgt?" (Delitzsch: *Commentar über die Genesis*, Leipzig, 1860, p. 101). "but if day is used figuratively, evening and morning must likewise be" (John D. Davis: *Genesis and Semitic Tradition*, London, 1894, p. 17).

the language suggests that the vegetation came forth from the earth as it does today. This point, however, cannot be pressed.

9. The purpose of the six days is to show how God, step by step, changed the uninhabitable and unformed earth of verse two into the well ordered world of verse thirty-one.[120]

10. The purpose of the first section of Genesis (1:1–2:3) is to exalt the eternal God as the alone Creator of heaven and earth, who in infinite wisdom and by the Word of his power brought the earth into existence and adorned and prepared it for man's habitancy. The section also prepares for the second portion of Genesis, the Generations, which deals with man's habitancy of God's world.

11. Genesis one is not poetry or saga or myth, but straight-forward, trustworthy history, and, inasmuch as it is a divine revelation, accurately records those matters of which it speaks. That Genesis one is historical may be seen from these considerations. 1) It sustains an intimate relationship with the remainder of the book. The remainder of the book (*i. e.*, The Generations) presupposes the Creation Account, and the Creation Account prepares for what follows. The two portions of Genesis are integral parts of the book and complement one another. 2) The characteristics of Hebrew poetry are lacking. There are poetic accounts of the creation and these form a striking contrast to Genesis one. 3) The New Testament regards certain events mentioned in Genesis one as actually having taken place. We may safely allow the New Testament to be our interpreter of this mighty first chapter of the Bible.

---

[120] One fact which Visée insists must be maintained in the study of Genesis one is "dat er ook een bepaalde volgorde was in dat werk Gods van ‚lager‘ tot ‚hoger‘, van ‚minder‘ tot ‚meer‘ samengesteld, waarbij elk volgend geschapene het eerder geschapene vooronderstelde" (*Lucerna*, p. 639).